Internet Projects for Primary

Creating a Web Site

Michael Strachan and Frances Thomas

A & C BLACK

The Authors: Michael Strachan and Frances Thomas are qualified teacher-trainers of Primary school teachers in the use of computers in schools.

Published 2002 by
A & C Black (Publishers) Limited
Alderman House
37 Soho Square
London WID 3QZ

ISBN 0-7136-5704-9

Acknowledgements
This book was produced for A & C Black by
Bender Richardson White, Uxbridge.

Project Editor: Lionel Bender
Designer: Malcolm Smythe
Art Editor: Ben White
Illustrations: Jim Robins
Production: Kim Richardson

Teachers' Notes and Photocopiable Activities created by: Lucy Poddington and Sue Neale

Cover illustration: Charlotte Hard

The authors have made every effort to trace the copyright holders of the screen shots used in this book to seek their permission to reproduce them. If any rights have been omitted, the authors offer their sincere apologies. In the event of an error or omission, please contact the publisher for correction at reprint. The authors have also taken every care to ensure that the instructions and web site addresses contained in this book are accurate and up-to-date. The authors are not responsible for the content of any web site listed nor are they responsible for any offensive or inaccurate material contained within them.

Microsoft®, Microsoft logo, Microsoft Windows®, Microsoft Internet Explorer®, Microsoft FrontPage® and Microsoft Notepad® are registered trademarks of Microsoft Corporation in the United States and other countries. Netscape®, Netscape logo, Netscape Navigator® and Netscape N logo are registered trademarks of Netscape Communications Corporation in the United States and other countries. Apple®, Apple logo and Macintosh® are trademarks of Apple Computer, Inc., registered in the United States and other countries. CuteFTP® and CuteHTML® are registered trademarks of GlobalSCAPE, Inc. in the United States and other countries. Textease® is a registered trademark of Softease Limited. HotDog PageWiz® is a registered trademark of Sausage Software. Screenshots reproduced with the permission of Microsoft Corporation and Apple Computer Inc. The National Curriculum is copyright Her Majesty's Stationery Office 2001.

Every effort has been made to attribute copyright correctly.

A CIP catalogue record for this book is available from the British Library.

Printed in Great Britain

CONTENTS

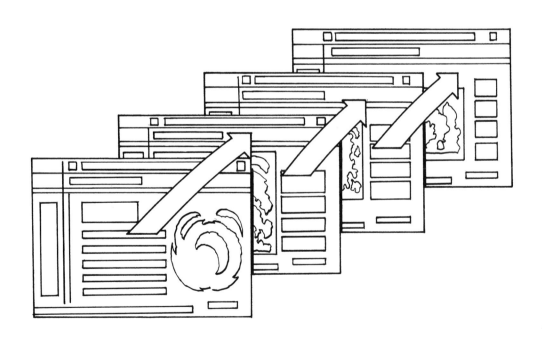

ABOUT THIS BOOK

This book is a practical guide for teachers who would like to set up or improve a school web site and involve children in planning and creating web pages for other teachers, parents and other children to see. It has been written by teachers with the help of Literacy and ICT educational advisors. It is a resource to help both adults and children build up confidence and skills in Information and Communication Technology across the National Curriculum. Material is organised and explained in a practical way, using non-technical language. Where technical terms cannot be avoided, they are explained in the Glossary on pages 93–95.

If you are a Key Stage 2 classroom teacher or newly qualified, this book will show you how you can contribute to a school web site and involve your class.

If you are an ICT co-ordinator, you will find ideas to help you set up a web site for your school, as well as train and support less-experienced colleagues.

If you are a trainee teacher, you will find the practical classroom advice valuable as you build up your repertoire of teaching skills and expand your understanding.

If you are a parent who wants to take an active role helping your child through the maze of the World Wide Web, then this book will help you support your child's teachers in promoting the best use of web sites as learning tools.

Creating a Web Site aims to make sense of the World Wide Web and show you how it can be an important part of teaching and learning. The book focuses on *Windows* PCs running *Internet Explorer* software but can be used with *Netscape Navigator* software and Apple Macintosh or Research Machines computers.

BOOKS TO MAKE SENSE OF THE INTERNET

At first, trying to get into cyberspace can be daunting. There is a lot of jargon, and the technology keeps changing. The basics, however, are not that difficult to grasp. *Creating a Web Site* is one of three ICT titles, produced by teachers for teachers, about making the best educational use of the Internet. Each title has more than 30 photocopiable activity sheets.

The other two titles are:
Finding Information Practical aspects of getting on the World Wide Web, searching for information and downloading text and graphics for educational projects.

Using E-Mail Practical aspects of using e-mail to communicate with people and organisations around the world.

SECTION 1: INTRODUCTION

The introduction contains background information about school web sites: what they can be used for, how they can be set up and put on the World Wide Web, and how to make the best educational use of them. There is a brief summary of the Government's requirements for teaching Information and Communication Technology in schools and how creating school web sites can be part of this.

SECTION 2: PLANNING AND CREATING A SCHOOL WEB SITE – THE BASICS

This section provides a step-by-step guide to planning and building a school web site. There are diagrams, computer screen shots and a minimum of text. Many pages give practical hints and tips. The section includes features on designing a web site, using web-authoring software, and uploading a web site onto the World Wide Web. Web-authoring packages come with their own detailed software manuals and tutorial programs. Here, we provide an overview of the main kinds of packages and how they differ.

SECTION 3: QUESTIONS AND ANSWERS

This section answers some frequently-asked questions, such as 'How secure is a school web site?' and addresses copyright issues. It also describes the hardware and software you will need to create a web site and get online.

SECTION 4: PHOTOCOPIABLE PROJECTS

Photocopiable activity sheets provide teachers with activities for children to do in classroom groups or individually. They offer structured lessons that encourage children to plan, design and write their own web pages. The activities provide focused tasks that encourage critical thinking and practice in ICT-related skills. They also encourage children to create material for their school web site.

At the start of the section are Teachers' Notes. These give ideas and suggestions for making the most of the activities.

Most of the activity sheets end with a challenge, called 'Next Step', which reinforces and extends the children's learning and provides the teacher with an opportunity for assessment. These more challenging activities might be appropriate for only a few children. The activities cover a wide range of curriculum subjects and are pitched at different learning levels. Some can be carried out away from the computer. Others are designed to be completed by using the Internet. The activities can also be carried out at home.

SECTION 5: RECOMMENDED WEB SITES

This part of the book lists recommended web sites and links that teachers have found especially useful.

SECTION 6: AT-A-GLANCE GUIDES

Finally there are web site planning sheets that can be photocopied and used by teachers and children, and a glossary.

5

SECTION 1:
INTRODUCTION

WHAT IS A SCHOOL WEB SITE?

A school web site is an information store and retrieval centre created by teachers, pupils and parents for use by people both inside and outside the school. It is one of millions of web sites on the Internet – the worldwide network of computers that can share information using telephone lines and cables.

Web sites are created by individuals and organisations on their computers. A web site consists of an assembly of 'web pages', each of which can be accessed on a computer screen. All you need to do is to connect your computer to the Internet and either key in the unique 'address' of the web site you want to explore or use a 'search engine' directory that will give you a choice of web sites to choose from.

Creating and using a school web site opens up opportunities for the whole school to work together and, at the same time, learn how to handle and communicate information in new ways. Furthermore, children will be able to display their work not only within the school but to parents, the local community and other schools nationwide and in other countries. Their work can include not only text but, if desired, also images, music, sounds and videos. For example, a school web site can contain photographs of the school buildings; a noticeboard of staff meetings and parents' evenings; samples of the pupils' work; and video footage of the school play or a special outing.

WHAT DOES A SCHOOL WEB SITE OFFER?

A well-organised and maintained school web site can be used in the following ways:

- to advertise the school to the local community and wider world

- as an electronic school prospectus

- to keep staff informed about changes to timetables and classroom allocations

- to inform school governors and parents about meetings.

- to inform parents about school activities such as plays, outings, sports events and summer trips

- to inform pupils about teachers' absences or special activities in the school, such as after-school clubs or revision classes

- to introduce children to the Internet and the World Wide Web

- as an educational tool to help teach Information and Communication Technology (ICT), Literacy, Numeracy, and other National Curriculum subjects

- as a noticeboard and diary for dates of school holidays and events

- as a showcase for pupils' work and achievements

- as a summary of lessons so that parents of children on long absences through illness can help their children study at home or in hospital

- to provide links to other web sites dealing with, for example, the National Curriculum, educational television programmes, educational books, local museums and local libraries

- to share experiences and interests with other schools in this country and abroad.

A school web site can provide a tremendous opportunity to show off the school's academic, sporting and cultural achievements. It is the ideal place to publish the results of Standard Attainment Tests (SATs), the end of Key Stage testing results, and the outcome of Ofsted inspections. These can be accompanied by a commentary on how the school is achieving these results and its plans for the future.

As a parent, visiting the web site can offer a greater sense of involvement and partnership with the school. You can find out what is happening in the classrooms, see your child's work on display and feel more involved in the life of the school. The school web site can also provide e-mail links with the head teacher and staff.

For pupils, helping to create the school web site is an opportunity to be involved in the running of the school and to contribute to its activities. It can improve their self-esteem and establish team skills and working relationships with adults and other children.

Once the school web site is established, pupils can display on it their classroom work or stories, articles, photographs and other material that they produce at home and bring into school. Publishing on the web site encourages children to work creatively and challenges them to structure their knowledge in an easily understandable way.

Opposite are examples of pages from school web sites to illustrate some of these uses:

HINTS AND TIPS

If you are starting a school web site from scratch, don't be too ambitious at first. Start by using the site as a noticeboard for timetables, lesson changes and information about the curriculum. As you and your colleagues become more experienced on the computer and in using web-site-building software, then invite the children and parents to participate in planning the site, adding new web pages and publishing material on the site.

INTERNET SECURITY

Having your school web site on the Internet makes your school more public. Take steps to ensure no sensitive information is put on the site – for example, teachers' home addresses, telephone numbers and e-mail addresses. Also, be sure that children in school do not have unsupervised access to the Internet.

For more information on Internet security see Section 3.

A web page from Ambleside Primary School web site. It offers links to other pages on the site and to other web sites. It features many pages of children's work.
www.ambleside.schoolzone.co.uk

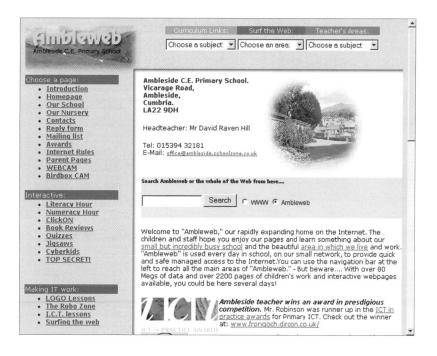

Introductory, or 'home page' of Christ Church Primary School, Battersea, London. There are four main links to other areas of the web site.
schoolsite.edex.net.uk/333

This is a page from an Internet site that has been created to link schools across Europe. It includes some good ideas for web pages and links.
www.eun.org

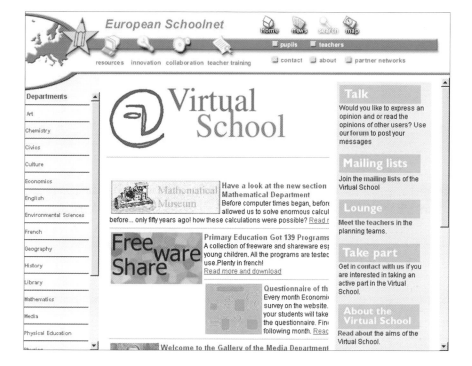

How does a School Web Site Work?

A web site consists of a collection of 'web pages' made up of text and images put together using a special piece of computer software called a web-authoring program. Each page holds and displays a full screen of information.

Within each page, there are usually several 'hot spots' or 'hypertext links'. These are buttons, images or words or phrases highlighted in colour or underlined that act as links to other pages or to other web sites. When you move the computer mouse over a hot spot or hypertext link, the cursor on the screen changes from a pointer to a hand symbol. Clicking the mouse button takes you directly to the new web page or web site.

HINTS AND TIPS

We have used *Internet Explorer* because most computers come with this software already installed. Browsers, like any other software package, are regularly updated and improved. We have used version 5.5, which is the latest version at the time of writing. This book can be used with earlier versions and will still be usable with upgraded versions.

There are other excellent browsers such as *Netscape Navigator.*

Wherever possible, use the latest version. It will have been improved to get rid of any bugs and is likely to be smoother and give less trouble.

A WEB SITE

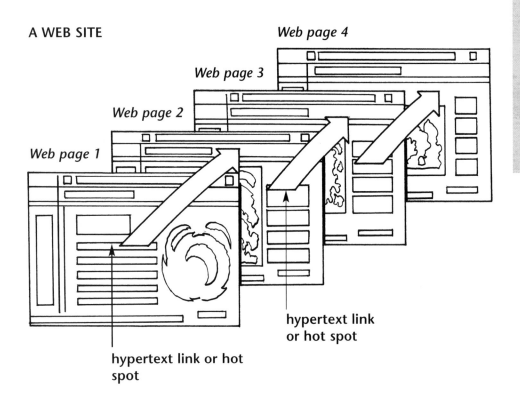

Web page 4

Web page 3

Web page 2

Web page 1

hypertext link or hot spot

hypertext link or hot spot

Every web site has its own Internet address called a Universal Resource Locator (URL). Using the 'web browser' – Internet-searching software such as *Internet Explorer* or *Netscape Navigator* – installed on your computer, you type in the address of the school web site you want to access.

Suppose you want to go to the web site of a hypothetical school, Manor School. Type in http://www.manorschool.ac.uk, click on the 'GO' button or press the ENTER key on your keyboard and up comes the introductory page of the Manor School web site. This page is called the 'home page'. Links from here will take you to individual pages within the site.

The way the pages of a web site are linked together makes up a network like a spider's web. Hence, a diagram showing these links is called a spidergram. Below, we show the spidergram for our Manor School web site. Each box represents a different area of the web site. An area can have one or more web pages.

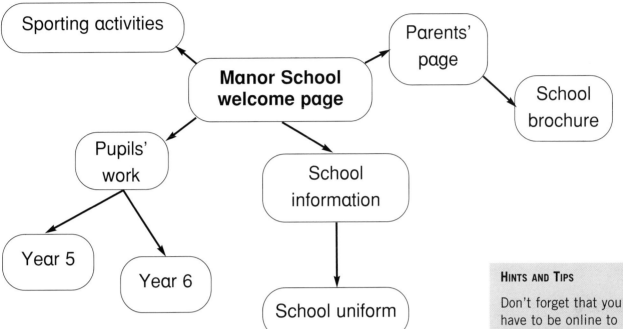

HYPERTEXT MARKUP LANGUAGE

Underlying every web site and each web page is a special computer language called HTML, or Hypertext Markup Language. This gives instructions to the browser software telling it how to display the items on the computer screen or which Internet address to go to next. HTML also forms the hot spots or hypertext links that create the spidergram.

HTML looks complicated and daunting to use. However, most of the software packages used to create web sites – known as 'web-authoring' packages – handle the HTML instructions for you. It is certainly possible to create and manage a web site without ever knowing how to use HTML.

For more on HTML see pages 21–22 and page 41. The different types of web-authoring packages are summarised on pages 22–24 and are looked at in more detail on pages 35–42.

For more on HTML see pages 21–22 and page 41. The different types of web-authoring packages are summarised on pages 22–24 and are looked at in more detail on pages 35–42.

HINTS AND TIPS

Don't forget that you have to be online to access a web site.

Type the URL carefully (check upper and lower cases and spaces), exactly as it should be written.

Do not be put off if the browser appears to be trying to finish the address for you. It is an 'intuitive' piece of software and stores commonly used web site addresses.

TECHNICAL NOTES

What the suffix letters mean:

.ac	academic/educational
.co	company
.com	commercial
.gov	government
.org	organisation
.net	internet company

WEB SITES AND THE NATIONAL CURRICULUM

Creating and using web sites is part of Information and Communication Technology (ICT), which is a foundation subject in the National Curriculum. This means that it is expected to be at the heart of the educational process and used wherever it is appropriate and helpful.

The Government has published its blueprint for the Internet and Education for the new millennium. It describes the World Wide Web as a 'mosaic of interconnected sites', including:

- commercial content-providers

- academic sites with educational resources developed for the classroom

- web sites designed by schools.

Much of the curriculum information from the Department for Education and Employment (DfEE) and the Qualifications and Curriculum Authority (QCA) is already online. You can visit the DfEE and QCA web sites at:

> www.dfee.gov.uk
> www.qca.org.uk

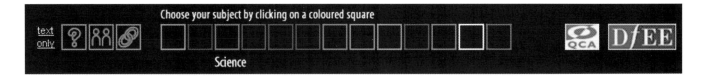

Welcome to National Curriculum online

And welcome to a new site. It links to hundreds of useful websites that will help you to teach the National Curriculum for England, linked to teaching requirements. Your expertise is stored and shared here, because useful websites can be rated by teachers - the most popular rise to the top of search results. At the moment there are around 190 sites to cover the whole of the National Curriculum, and more are being added every day. In the near future the Schemes of Work will be linked to the National Curriculum programmes of study in the same way. You will also find tools to help you search the curriculum by theme, such as key skills.

To grow, this site will need teachers' help. Do you know of a good web site you'd like to submit? Or if you publish an educational website, would you like it to be linked to this site?

You will need Netscape 4 or Microsoft IE 4 (or higher) to use this site.

To explore the new features this site offers, click on any subject in the navigation bar at the top of this page, or on Learning across the curriculum.

About this site
What's new and coming soon
How to use this site
How to print
Downloadable files
Recommend a resource
Link your resource to this site
Comments and contacts

Curriculum aims and values

How the National Curriculum works

General teaching requirements

Non-statutory guidelines for ...
PSHE and citizenship at key stages 1&2
PSHE at key stages 3&4
MFL at key stage 2

Other sites Teachernet Learning Journey UK online | Buy a copy © HMSO Designed by C21 | Northern Ireland Scotland Wales

Designing and/or building a web site offers a wide range of teaching and learning opportunities. It provides a stimulating focus for acquiring and practising skills in Literacy, Design and Technology, and Art and Design. It engages children in critical thinking and problem-solving in real contexts, and provides children with opportunities to participate confidently and more fully in the school and the wider community.

The statement of the National Curriculum Information and Communication Technology requirements for Key Stage 2 is shown below. Communicating information over the Internet through well-designed school web sites can contribute to fulfilling many of the statements. The most relevant statements are underlined.

From the National Curriculum:
> *'During Key Stage 2 pupils use a wider range of ICT tools and information sources to support their work in other subjects. They develop their research skills and decide what information is appropriate for their work. They begin to question the plausibility and quality of information. They learn how to amend their work and present it in a way that suits its audience.'*

These requirements are divided into five areas:
1. **Knowledge, skills and understanding**
2. **Developing ideas and making things happen**
3. **Exchanging and sharing information**
4. **Reviewing, modifying and evaluating work as it progresses**
5. **Breadth of study**

1. **Knowledge, skills and understanding**
   PUPILS SHOULD BE TAUGHT:
   a to talk about what information they need and how they can find and use it (for example, searching the Internet or a CD-ROM, using printed material, asking people);
   b how to prepare information for development using ICT, including selecting suitable sources, finding information, classifying it and checking it for accuracy (for example, finding information from books or newspapers, creating a class database, classifying by characteristics and purposes, checking the spelling of names is consistent);
   c to interpret information, to check it is relevant and reasonable and to think about what might happen if there were any errors or omissions.

2. **Developing ideas and making things happen**
   PUPILS SHOULD BE TAUGHT:
   a how to develop and refine ideas by bringing together, organising and reorganising text, tables, images and sound as appropriate (for example, desktop publishing, multimedia presentations);

13

From the National Curriculum (continued):

b how to create, test, improve and refine sequences of instructions to make things happen, and to monitor events and respond to them (for example, monitoring changes in temperature, detecting light levels and turning on a light);

c to use simulations and explore models in order to answer 'What if . . .?' questions, to investigate and evaluate the effect of changing values and to identify patterns and relationships (for example, simulation software, spreadsheet models).

3. Exchanging and sharing information

PUPILS SHOULD BE TAUGHT:

a how to share and exchange information in a variety of forms, including e-mail (for example, displays, posters, animations, musical compositions);

b to be sensitive to the needs of the audience and think carefully about the content and quality when communicating information (for example, work for presentation to other pupils, writing for parents, publishing on the Internet).

4. Reviewing, modifying and evaluating work as it progresses

PUPILS SHOULD BE TAUGHT TO:

a review what they and others have done, to help them develop their ideas;

b describe and talk about the effectiveness of their work with ICT, comparing it with other methods and considering the effect it has on others (for example, the impact made by a desktop-published newsletter or poster);

c talk about how they could improve future work.

5. Breadth of study

DURING THE KEY STAGE, pupils should be taught the knowledge, skills and understanding through:

a working with a range of information to consider its characteristics and purposes (for example, collecting factual data from the Internet and a class survey to compare the findings);

b working with others to explore a variety of information sources and ICT tools (for example, searching the Internet for information about a different part of the world, designing textile patterns using graphics software, using ICT tools to capture and change sounds);

c investigating and comparing the uses of ICT inside and outside school.

MAKING USE OF THE SCHOOL WEB SITE IN THE CLASSROOM

Typically, a school web site is built and maintained by the school's ICT co-ordinator with the help of pupils, staff and parents. If your school already has a web site, you and your pupils can improve on it, update it and add to it, or use it as a source of information. Otherwise, you can create the school web site from scratch

CREATING A SCHOOL WEB SITE FROM SCRATCH

This is a long-term process requiring a large investment of time and energy on the part of everyone involved. But it is a great opportunity for teachers, children, parents, school governors and others to work together to create a resource that everyone can use and share. Planning a school web site is the kind of activity that fits in well to the last summer term of Year 6, with pupils from Year 5 preparing themselves to take over the running and redesign in the following year.

To create a school web site from scratch, you will need to have basic computer skills and become familiar with a web-authoring program and the software that allows you to place the school web site on the Internet.

Regarding content for the web site, most of the basic information about the school and teachers already exists in the school prospectus and other documents. If this information is not already on the school computer, it can be scanned in or keyed in by the staff. Additional information or material can be obtained from the Internet or specially created for the site, giving an opportunity for teachers, children and parents to contribute. Here are some ways for following up research on the Internet:

- Make and maintain a list or chart of search engines and particularly useful or interesting web sites to be used in your classroom, with notes about their suitability for particular subjects and topics.

- Download and copy pictures/music/sound/video excerpts into suitable software such as *Powerpoint* or *Textease* to produce simple slide shows or project packs.

- Save and store simple information/pages for others to use in various projects.

- Compile topic books/news-sheets for other audiences.

- Collaboratively produce topic questionnaires for others to use. These can be for any subject.

- Groups can compile reports on selected aspects of a topic, for example Tudor food and drink, fashion, or houses and homes.

HINTS AND TIPS

With any new software such as a web-authoring package, it is a good idea to practise using it before you involve the children and parents. Your ICT teacher co-ordinator will be able to help you.

For further information on web-authoring packages, turn to pages 22–24 and 35–42.

IMPROVING AN EXISTING SCHOOL WEB SITE

The first thing you and the children can do is improve the web site's content – perhaps amending existing pages with updated ideas or adding new material, as described earlier. In this context, the web site can become the focus of ICT classwork. It involves the children using basic computer-handling skills, word processing, desktop publishing, data handling and manipulating graphics.

Redesigning a school web site requires children to think about how their work will look when it is displayed on screen rather than being printed out on sheets of A4 paper. It can involve children in looking at examples of other school web sites and becoming critically aware of the features that make some sites stand out from the rest.

PUBLISHING CHILDREN'S WORK ON THE WEB SITE

Displaying children's work on the web site encourages pupils to work creatively but in a logical, structured way. Creating content for the web site is an activity that can be done by children starting in Year 3 or 4. Following guidelines from the teacher, they can start by writing short stories and poems, then progress to structuring text into newspaper-like articles or creating simple graphics. Later, they can create their own ideas for web pages and, with the help of the ICT co-ordinator, see how these are placed on the web site.

A good way to inspire children to produce their own work for the web site is to give them a wider sense of purpose. Making resources for other pupils, teachers, parents and other schools to use and look at can fulfil that purpose. It will also add to the children's self-esteem to feel that they are web authors.

The kinds of work the children can put on the web site are:

- short stories or poems they have written
- their book or film reviews
- articles they have created about topics discussed in the classroom
- quizzes, puzzles or simple games they have created
- notices for meetings or activities at school
- results of school sports events
- photographs and stories about their holidays or school outings
- reports of local events
- requests to other pupils or to parents to bring in materials for school events or displays.

HINTS AND TIPS

The ICT curriculum from the Department for Education and Employment (DfEE) and the Qualifications and Curriculum Authority (QCA) is available online.

You can visit the DfEE and QCA web sites at:

www.dfee.gov.uk
www.qca.org.uk

USING THE SCHOOL WEB SITE AS A LINK TO OTHER SITES

One of the major functions of a school web site can be to provide links for pupils, teachers, parents and governors to other important web sites. Within the school web pages, there can be hypertext links, or hot spots, taking you to:

- national government sites that give details of the National Curriculum, Schemes of Work, and Standards
- local government sites containing contact names and addresses of local schools, colleges, educational advisors and educational support groups
- computer software manufacturers that provide free, teach-yourself lessons, revision courses and upgrades of the school's software packages over the Internet
- educational sites giving advice and support to teachers and parents on using computers in the classroom
- other schools – local, national and international
- educational resource sites that offer a range of cross-curricular ideas and resources for use in school and at home
- local and national libraries, art galleries and museums
- newspapers
- educational television channels and radio stations
- educational book publishers and other suppliers of classroom resources and home-learning materials
- reference-book publishers who have made available, free on the Internet, encyclopedias, dictionaries and other reference works
- advice and support centres for parents
- organisations dealing with children with special needs such as deafness, blindness, dyslexia.

Everyone in the school, and parents, can be involved in recommending and selecting web sites for inclusion as school web site links. Check out any sites before adding them. As a classroom activity, you can get the children to regularly review these sites. The process of maintaining web site links, adding good ones and deleting bad ones, can be incorporated into classroom and year group planning activities.

LINKS PAGE OF CHRIST CHURCH PRIMARY SCHOOL'S WEB SITE
schoolsite.edex.net.uk/333

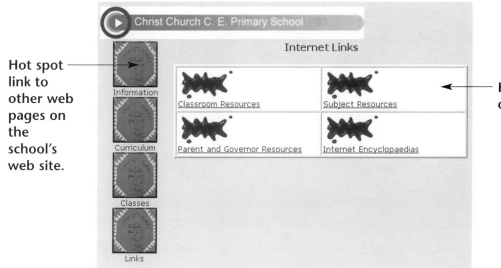

Hot spot link to other web pages on the school's web site.

Hot spot link to other web sites.

A school web site can also act as an 'Intranet' – an internal school network of ideas, information and resources. Having pages on the site that all classes have access to and can modify is often the way in which a school web site is developed until it is ready to be uploaded and shown off to the outside world.

Links on the school web site can provide teachers and pupils with information, advice and communication with the world outside the school. They can also be sources of text, images, graphics, sounds and video material that can be downloaded and then used in classroom work, homework, displays or presentations such as the school web site itself.

BASIC COMPUTER SKILLS AND EQUIPMENT

Before attempting to create a school web site, you need to be comfortable with some basic computer 'household management'.

You need to:

- know your way around the external parts of a computer system – how they are connected and what functions they perform

- have basic mouse and keyboard skills

- have word-processing skills

- be able to find your way around the desktop

- feel comfortable managing files and folders and moving and sizing windows for comfortable working on screen

- be able to copy, save, move and delete files

- be able to troubleshoot basic printer problems such as paper jams and carry out routine maintenance

- feel confident accessing the Internet and using your browser and search engines

- be familiar with the basics of the software you will use to put your school web site on the Internet.

All the software recommended and featured later in this book is user-friendly and well supported by online tutorials. If you are a teacher, then your LEA is likely to run courses on web-building. There are also many courses at local colleges or run online and face-to-face by private companies.

HINTS AND TIPS

Downloading and using resources will involve important issues of copyright (see pages 27 and 45). Nevertheless, including such links will save teachers, pupils and parents considerable time searching the Internet.

The school web site is accessible from any computer, at all times and from anywhere. So it can be an invaluable help for pupils forced to work at home or in hospital or who are trying to catch up on work they may have missed.

COMPUTER EQUIPMENT

Many Primary schools and most homes are equipped with stand-alone computers, that is, computers that are not linked by cables to any other computer. An increasing number of schools and some homes have networked computers. This means that one machine acts as a server (host). The host computer is connected all the time to the Internet. It stores and relays the software and web site information to the other computers in the network.

Whether stand-alone or networked, if a computer has a modem – a unit connected to a telephone line that provides a link to the Internet – and the appropriate web-authoring software, it can be used to create a school web site.

If you want to practise web-authoring or view the school web site from home and you have not yet got your own computer, here are some guidelines to help you choose the ideal machine.

- First, you need to decide whether to buy a personal computer (PC) running *Windows* software, or an Apple Macintosh computer (usually shortened to just Apple Mac, Apple or Mac). It is best to have the same type of computer at home as you or your children use at school.

- Look for a PC or Mac with a modem and the largest hard disk you can afford. The hard disk is where you store programs and the files you create. It needs to be at least 4 gigabytes (Gb) and preferably more.

- You also need short-term memory power called random-access memory (RAM). You need at least 128 Mb RAM to deal with big images, video or DVD files.

- You will probably find it cheapest and easiest to buy a computer package, with central processing unit, monitor, keyboard, mouse, printer and other accessories bundled together These packages usually come with a comprehensive range of software. A scanner and digital camera are useful extras. The illustration on page 20 shows a complete package. Look for special offers in computer shops or advertised in the national press.

SOFTWARE AND AN INTERNET SERVICE PROVIDER (ISP)

School computers will already have word-processing and graphics packages. A home computer will need these for creating and storing material to go on the school web site. You can buy them at any good computer store.

Most school and home computers will not have a web-authoring program or the software needed to put the school web site on the Internet. The latter is known as File Transfer Protocol (FTP) software. You will need to buy and install these.

HINTS AND TIPS

If you are buying your own equipment, make sure you have an on-site support contract.

Get at least a 17" monitor, for an easier display.

Choose a computer that has as much hard disk capacity as you can afford.

TECHNICAL NOTES

The processor is the microchip at the heart of any computer. The speed at which it processes information is measured in megahertz (MHz). The higher the number, the faster the computer goes. Your computer needs at least 600 MHz to give you fast access to the Internet.

An internal modem is the box that connects you to the Internet. The speed at which the modem connects you is measured in kilobytes per second (Kbps) – the faster the connection, the better.

19

A COMPUTER SYSTEM

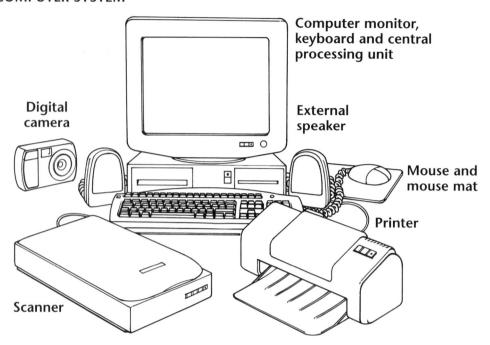

Computer monitor, keyboard and central processing unit

Digital camera

External speaker

Mouse and mouse mat

Printer

Scanner

Ask your school computer supplier or local computer store for guidance on which to buy. We have listed the different types of web-authoring programs on pages 21–23.

To gain access to the Internet, you will need to be signed up with an Internet Service Provider (ISP). This is a company that provides a connection to the Internet via a telephone line and probably also supplies the software needed to search the Internet and use e-mail. The ISP will usually also provide space on the Internet for storing the school's web site.

Schools are usually contracted with an ISP during purchase and installation. Individuals may find an ISP connection already set up on the computer they buy. If you are choosing an ISP to use at home, select one of the major companies. If you are connected to a cable TV company, investigate their Internet provision.

PREPARING TO USE THE SCHOOL WEB SITE

As the first step in creating a school web site, you should set up an editorial and design team of representatives from each group of people involved. This should probably include the headteacher, the school secretary, the ICT co-ordinator, one or two teachers and parents, a school governor and a selection of pupils across the age range. The planning team should draw up a questionnaire for all teachers, parents and pupils to establish what the school web site should include, how it should look and who will provide all the text and graphics needed. We have included a basic school web site questionnaire in the Web Site Planner in Section 6.

HINTS AND TIPS

Here are some questions to consider when choosing an ISP:

● Is there a monthly fee or annual subscription? If so, is it expensive?

● Are there extra charges for being online? Will these be prohibitive?

● Does the company provide a CD-ROM with pre-configured connection software for your computer?

● Is there readily available, free telephone support? If not, how much time and money will you spend getting help?

● Will your ISP host your school web site?

Before using a school web site in the classroom, you need to plan your lessons in advance and to record their outcomes. Your school probably already has a documented system for recording details of planning, delivery, follow-up and assessment of curriculum activities. If not, then a simple form like the one shown below may be helpful.

site TRAINING

ICT Activity Preparation and Planning

The Adobe Acrobat version of this form is directly linked to the sites shown...

www.adobe.com Get Acrobat Reader

Year Group: ____________ Topic: ____________

Date: ____________ Teacher: ____________

www.qca.org.uk QCA

QCA requirements

NOTES

QCA

Briefly record these by downloading directly if you are using the Adobe .pdf version ...or copy & paste...

PREPARATION

Note the details of resources, URLs and introductory activities away from the computer...

DELIVERY

Note the details such as physical organisation, introduction and conclusion AND alternative activity off the computers...

FOLLOW-UP

What went well, what did not, what could be changed? PLUS classroom activities for sharing and displaying children's ICT work...

HINTS AND TIPS

Finding time for the school web site team to meet can be problematic: it will probably be best to meet after school, at the weekend or even during the school holidays.

HINTS AND TIPS

If it is too much work for your school to move its existing classroom preparation and planning documentation online, consider using the example shown here, which exists in the program *Adobe Acrobat* online format.

The planning document should cover all the National Curriculum requirements, the classroom preparations, how the lesson/activity was delivered or carried out, what follow-up took place back in the classroom and a brief assessment of the process.

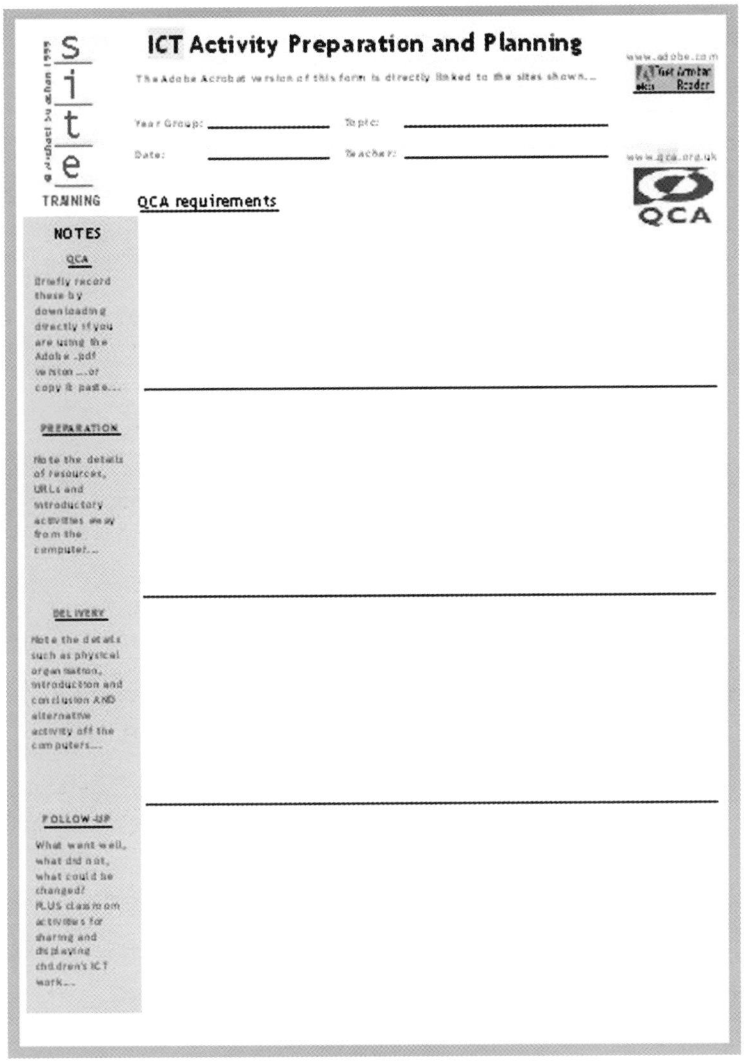

CHOOSING WEB-AUTHORING SOFTWARE

Web-authoring software comes in many shapes and sizes ranging from desktop publisher packages with added HTML features to huge professional packages. There are four main types of software you should consider: 1. Template editors. 2. WYSIWYG editors. 3. Markup editors. 4. Block editors.

As mentioned on page 11, underlying all web-authoring packages is the computer language HTML. It puts 'tags' around each piece of text, individual picture or hot spot so that the browser software (*Intenet Explorer* or *Netscape Navigator*) knows where to find it and how to display it on the screen. However, three of the types of packages we recommend do not require that you learn this – they automatically translate your instructions into HTML.

The image below shows the heading part of a typical school web site page and below it is the HTML instructions for the heading itself. The < symbol is the start or opening of a tag. The > symbol ends or closes the tag. The / symbol shows the bold and font instructions are finished.

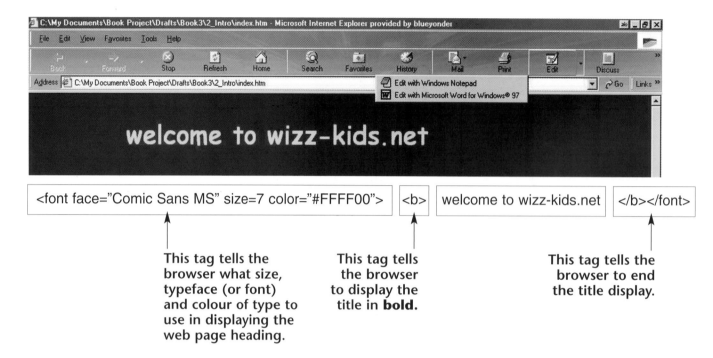

| <font face="Comic Sans MS" size=7 color="#FFFF00"> | <b> | welcome to wizz-kids.net | </b></font> |

This tag tells the browser what size, typeface (or font) and colour of type to use in displaying the web page heading.

This tag tells the browser to display the title in **bold**.

This tag tells the browser to end the title display.

For more examples of HTML tags, see page 41.

Below and on pages 23 and 24 is a summary of the four main types of web-authoring packages.

TEMPLATE EDITORS

These packages – such as *Microsoft Publisher 2000* – give you ready-made page templates and a range of options for design of buttons, backgrounds and headings. They include 'wizards' – sets of on-screen instructions that take you, step-by-step, through the options in building individual web pages and making hypertext links between pages.

Many schools start off with this type of package because it comes supplied and installed on the computers. The wizard choices can be restrictive after a while, and teachers may wish to use the 'Publisher' facility of the software for creating their own designs. This does, however, make the package more complex and difficult to use.

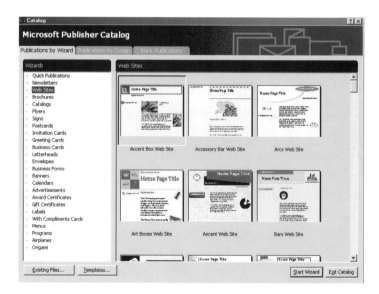

Microsoft Publisher screen, with web page templates.

WYSIWIG Editors

These include *Textease*, *Word* and *Front Page Express*. They work on the principle of 'What You See Is What You Get' – hence WYSIWIG – and are designed to be used by anyone no matter what their ICT experience. Within this category, the choices of design and layout are largely yours and, apart from the usual *Microsoft* 'Help' feature and the manuals that come with each software package, you are largely on your own.

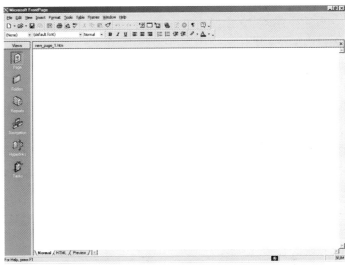

Front Page Express **screen, with web design toolbar and menu bar.**

What you place on screen is what you will expect to see on your web page. However, in practice some packages are better at doing this than others. *Textease* can be used for word-processing, desktop publishing and multimedia presentations, for setting up databases and spreadsheets and for web site-building.

Markup Editors

With a package such as *Notepad* – which comes free on every PC – you do not get any graphical display on the computer screen. Everything is displayed in HyperText Markup Language. This means that you really do need to know a good deal about tags and how to insert them. If you want to see what HTML looks like in practice, go to any web page on the Internet and click the 'Edit' button.

Another Markup editor is *CuteHTML*, which displays the text and tags in different colours and has a good instruction manual and a 'Help' facility built in.

Notepad **screen, with HTML language displayed.**

Block Editors

A good example among these packages is *Hotdog PageWiz*. It uses a simplified set of editing and formatting functions to create parts of a web page or 'blocks'. Each block, whether it is text, a graphic, banner heading or a dividing line, can be placed in any position on the screen and the appearance of the page can be adjusted.

With a block editor, you can switch from an editing page to one where the web version is displayed, to check your progress. The instruction manual and online tutorials are very helpful.

Hotdog PageWiz starter page, with menu and tool bars and windows for web page folders.

UPLOADING THE SCHOOL WEB SITE

Once you have completed your web site design, you will need to put your site on the Internet. To do this, you will need FTP (File Transfer Protocol) software. There is more about this in Section 3.

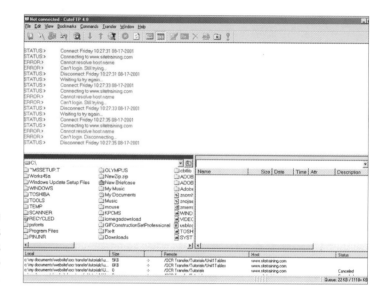

CuteFTP page, with menu and tool bars and windows showing folders and status of uploading a web site to the Internet.

CLASSROOM RESOURCES – BEFORE YOU START CREATING THE SITE

The usual classroom equipment – books, paper and pencils – are essential tools to use in the design stage when producing templates on which all the web site pages will be based. It is better to argue over a paper template and come to some kind of agreement before putting anything on the computer screen. This is especially important if you are considering designing from scratch or seriously redesigning an existing set of web pages.

We have included photocopiable activities in Section 4 of this book, and photocopiable web site plans in Section 6, to enable you, your pupils and colleagues to plan layouts on paper first.

SECTION 2:
PLANNING, BUILDING AND UPLOADING – THE BASICS

PART 1: PRE-PUBLISHING

Getting Started

To place and maintain your school web site on the Internet, your school must have an ISP, or Internet Service Provider. This is a company that 'hosts' your site by providing the necessary space on one of its powerful computers known as 'servers'. The company that provided your school with its computer equipment probably set up the ISP link for you. The ISP will provide you with some software on CD-ROM to allow you to go online to search the Internet and send e-mails. The ISP will also advise you on how much space is available on its server for your web site.

CHOOSING A DOMAIN NAME

Before you start working on your web site, think about its name and address on the Internet. Your school's web site address should be short, easy to remember, and reflect who you are.

Your web address, or URL (Universal Resource Locator), will begin with the standard prefix http:// followed by your site's 'domain name', which identifies your web site. For your site, your domain name should be your school name plus the suffix sch. for school and uk for country of origin.

Most Educational Authorities are linked with a particular ISP and, in this case, it is the LEA which allocates each school a space and domain name. So, for example, if your school is Rayners Lane Primary, then www.raynerslaneprimary is the 'host name' part of your address. If your LEA is Harrow, then the rest of the domain name is harrow.sch.uk. The whole URL for your school site could be http://www.raynerslaneprimary.harrow.sch.uk

GETTING TOGETHER AN EDITORIAL BOARD

Discuss your ideas for the web site with your headteacher and together find representative teachers, pupils and, if you wish, parents and school governors who can help you plan the site, source material and monitor progress and quality. Building a school web site is a time-consuming and creative process, so do share the load.

FOCUSING ON YOUR AUDIENCE

You need to determine who you want to attract to your site and what you want to show them. At first, it may be advisable to limit your audience to teachers and pupils. Then, once you are happy with the content and the ease of access to your site and its pages, you can widen your audience to parents, governors and the local community.

HINTS AND TIPS

You need to check that no other school has already claimed your web site address. There are many Internet companies selling or leasing domain names and usually they operate a domain name checking service to see if your first choice has already been taken. Once your chosen name is approved, register and pay for at least one year's subscription.

E-MAIL ADDRESSES

As part of the package from the ISP, every pupil and staff member will have an e-mail address such as:

aspriggs@ raynerslanep.harrow.sch.uk

Remember that, if you have a school e-mail address, then you may only be able to access your e-mail from school.

Consider having a universal e-mail address, such as through web sites *Hotmail* or *Yahoo*, so that you can send and receive messages from any computer worldwide.

If you are updating an existing web site, consider how the school's needs may have changed since the site was first built and whether you need to re-focus on a wider or different audience.

DECIDING ON THE CONTENT
The purpose of your web site could be:

- Advertising school achievements: school brochure details, Ofsted reports, exam results, cultural and sporting achievements, community service, etc.

- Business: details of school facilities that may be of interest to the local community, such as the hiring of school premises during the summer holidays.

- Noticeboard information: calendar/diary of events, subject, topic or classwork details, homework, holiday work, recommended school suppliers, etc.

- Communication: to facilitate e-mail communication between the school and parents, other schools, suppliers, etc.

- Showcase: pupils' work, pictures, puzzles, etc.

- Educational: links to educational web sites, etc.

There are more detailed lists of content ideas on pages 7–8 and 17.

HANDLING CONTRIBUTORS
Use your web site editorial team to commission contributions, monitor the quality of input and check on copyright issues. Contributions can be created directly on the school computer or created by teachers, pupils and parents on home computers, then saved on to discs or CD-ROMs and transferred. Once the site is set up, the same people can help maintain the site. Some web pages may need to be updated monthly or even weekly, while others will need changing only once a term or perhaps once a year.

CLASSROOM PLANNING ACTIVITIES
With your pupils, look critically at a range of other school web sites. Determine which are the most interesting sites and why. Try to build any good points and ideas into your school web site.

Investigate how search engines find web sites based on keywords. Ask pupils to write a short introduction to your web site that incorporates keywords – school name, location, headteacher and key web site topics. These keywords will be incorporated into the part of the web site coding that identifies the site in a search.

Collect on the school computer text, images and photographs that the children might want to include on your web site. The children can place these resources in dedicated folders, ready to import into the web site.

HINTS AND TIPS

When evaluating other web sites, consider the following:

- Does the home page clearly show who the site represents and what its function is?

- Are all the pages well-designed?

- Is the text easy to read, clear, concise and without spelling mistakes?

- Does the site download quickly?

- Are there many hot spots and do all of them function well?

- Do the graphics and photographs enhance the site?

- Is the information accurate and up-to-date?

- Does the site offer more or better information than you can find in books and directories?

You can set up a dedicated folder for children's work as follows:

1 Create a main folder on the school computer's hard disk for the web site.

2 On the Menu Bar, choose *New* then *Folder* to create further sub-folders.

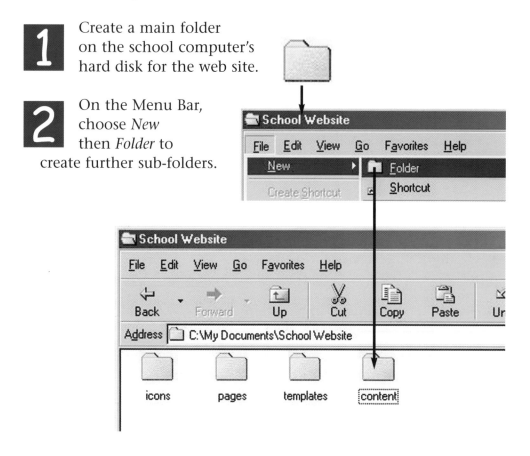

Choosing the Right Software

If your school already has a web site and is just looking to adapt and improve the existing web pages, look at the school's existing web-authoring package and see if its use can be extended. If it is restrictive, consider another more flexible package to do the job.

Beware that some web-authoring packages were designed for business rather than educational use. The software packages outlined on page 21 and featured in the following pages all focus on the educational aspects of web publishing. Which one you choose will depend on factors such as your current experience, your budget and how much time you can invest in what may be a completely new package for you.

To choose which File Transfer Protocol (FTP) software you need to upload your web site to the Internet, ask your ISP for advice or contact the ICT co-ordinators of other schools with web sites and review their experiences with different packages.

Web Page and Site Design

Using any web-authoring package, pages can be made up with a similar appearance and style. The easiest way to make sure all pages conform to your chosen design is first to create a template on which all the others will be based.

In planning a basic web site you will need to look at its shape and structure. Shape means how groups of web pages are linked to the index/home page. Structure means how the graphics and text blocks, fonts and colours are used across the individual pages.

SHAPE AND STRUCTURE

Most web sites now have an index/home page with landscape orientation which fits your monitor screen and contains links to other groups of pages. Also you will see that there are distinct areas on the pages which are very similar in appearance and position. This is a deliberate and very important design feature.

The way in which groups of web pages with similar content are structured and linked to the index/home page gives the whole site a shape which can be planned on paper.

PAGE SIZE AND BACKGROUND

Web-authoring packages work on a grid system like the cells of a spreadsheet. It can be helpful to plan the shape and structure of your web pages by using a template like those illustrated below.

As you can see, the template can be thought of as a series of imaginary blocks or sections surrounding the main text area.

The shaded parts show how some designers prefer to focus their pages, leading the eye to the central area.

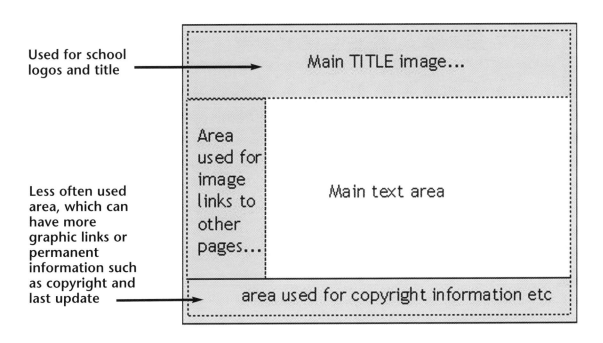

Used for school logos and title → **Main TITLE image...**

Area used for image links to other pages...

Main text area

Less often used area, which can have more graphic links or permanent information such as copyright and last update → area used for copyright information etc

ALIGNMENT

Alignment is the way different items or objects on the page, such as lines of text and pictures, are lined up with one another, as seen in these examples.

Main title and logo

Photograph forming link between heading and main text area. The centre of the photo is aligned with the centre of the heading.

Hot spot links aligned across the full width of the main text area.

Permanent information such as copyright details and last update. The text is centred in the bottom block of the page.

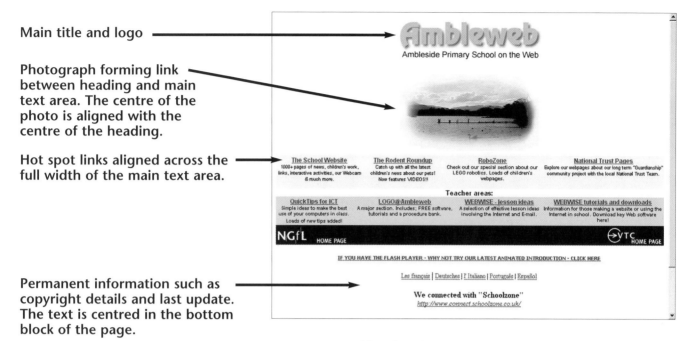

www.ambleside.schoolzone.co.uk

Whatever web-authoring package is used, it helps to have text and graphic resources stored in the folders prepared earlier on your hard disk, ready to use in creating a template.

Weak alignment leaves items placed irregularly and is distracting and tiring on the eye. So use strong alignment to make your pages look tidy.

Consider all the elements on the page, including the use of bullets, blocks of text and images. Alignment helps to simplify a page, making it easier to interpret and less irritating to the viewer.

An example from Our Lady and St Joseph Primary School, London N1, showing strong text and graphic alignment.
www.schoolwebsite.com

REPETITION

Using a template page makes it possible to create the other pages with the same general appearance. It is a good idea to keep the site logo, hot spot links and text on each page in the same positions. The exception is the first (Index/Home) page, which needs to be eye-catching.

CONTRAST

Differing text sizes and colours make interesting contrasts. Titles can be large, headings and body text smaller.

A dazzling array of colours may appeal to your artistic temperament but the effect on the viewer can be negative and fussy. So choose a few colours and do not mix them too much.

PROXIMITY

Placing related objects like hot spot links close to each other sounds like common sense and it helps the viewer make sense of the pages. Bear in mind that some web-authoring packages automatically group smaller objects into larger groups when converting to HTML – so leave large gaps between unrelated objects or those you wish to appear clearly separated.

On the curriculum pages of Christ Church Primary web site, the links bar on the left and the banner appear on each page. The curriculum 'splashes' link to subject pages. schoolsite.edex.net.uk/333

The title page of Roseburn Primary School site uses coloured text links on a strong background.

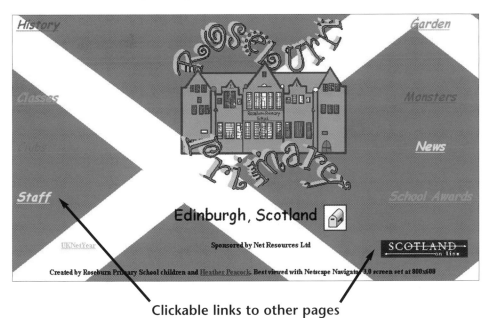

Clickable links to other pages

www.sol.co.uk/r/roseburn

PART 2: PUBLISHING

Starting Up on a Stand-Alone PC

When you switch on any computer – laptop or stand-alone – the screen will eventually settle down to something like the one shown below. The screen illustrated below is called the 'desktop'. If web-authoring software is installed on the computer, an active icon for the package will appear on the desktop.

DESKTOP

These small pictures are *active* icons – they are clickable short-cuts, which start applications or open files or folders.

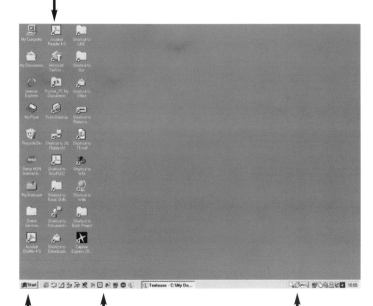

This is the *Start* button.

This is the *Task* bar – it also has short-cuts and shows applications currently running.

This is the *System tray*.

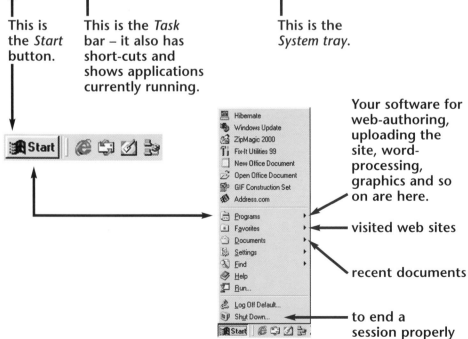

Your software for web-authoring, uploading the site, word-processing, graphics and so on are here.

visited web sites

recent documents

to end a session properly

1 These are three very important short-cuts on your desktop.

←—— 'My Computer' shows the hard disk (C), the floppy disk drive (A), the CD-ROM drive – usually (D) – and any extra drives.

'My Documents' is the area on your hard disk ←—— where your files and folders are stored.

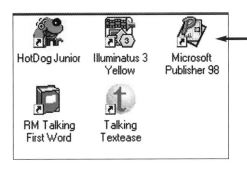

←—— *HotDog* and *Microsoft Publisher* are web-authoring programs. These icons are likely to be in a 'Communications' folder on your desktop. Click or double-click on one of these to get to your web site creation software.

Mouse Clicks

Command	Action
'select'	Click on an object with the left mouse button.
'double-click'	Move the pointer over the chosen object and, with the left mouse button, click twice in quick succession.
'right-click'	Click on an object with the right mouse button to view 'options'/ 'properties' – also to rename or delete.
'drag'	Move the pointer over the object to be dragged, hold down the left mouse button and move the object to its new location before releasing the button.

2 On a PC all data is displayed in windows like the one shown here from *HotDog PageWiz* web-authoring software. Each window has the same features.

maximise button

close button

minimise button

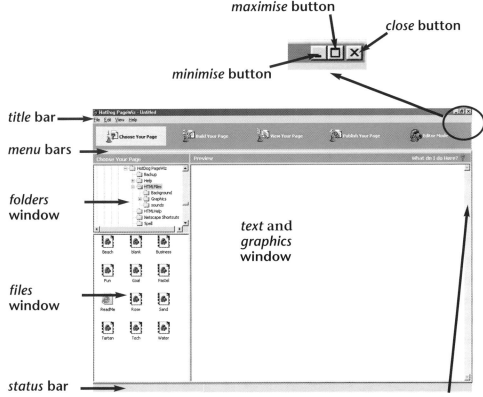

title bar

menu bars

folders window

text and *graphics* window

files window

status bar

scroll bar and *slider*

3 Always use the *Shut Down* option to close a session or restart.

Starting Up on a Network PC

HINTS AND TIPS

Type in your username and password carefully. You will have to start again if you misspell them, if you put in an extra space, or even if you use a capital letter where it should be lower case.

If your school has a network, every computer on it is connected to a central computer called a server. The server stores all the software and operating system and sends copies to all the networked machines.

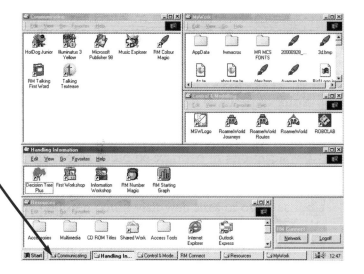

1 Once you have logged on to a network with your 'username' and password, a screen like this will appear.

2 To use a web-authoring program, look for the short-cut icons under *Communications*.

3 Clicking on the icon brings up the starter page of the software.

Starting Up on an Apple Mac

HINTS AND TIPS

The mouse used with an Apple Macintosh has only one button. Use a single click to highlight an icon and a double click to open or activate the icon or software.

Most primary schools use *Windows* PCs, so in this book we have focused on using these computers. If your school uses Apple Macintosh computers, the desktop and the opening screens for your web-authoring software will look different from those on a PC, but the step-by-step techniques for creating a web site are identical.

1 When you switch on an Apple Macintosh computer, the screen will settle down to look something like the one opposite. Double-click the mouse on the Macintosh Hard Drive icon to open the list of folders on your machine. Your web-authoring software is usually contained within the folder marked *Applications*.

2 Double-click on this folder to open your web-authoring software.

This is the *Hard Drive* icon

The *Apple* Icon is located here but a different icon may appear here temporarily depending on the software you are running.

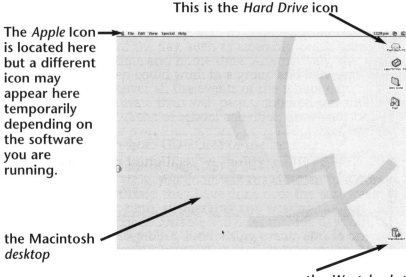

the Macintosh *desktop*

the *Wastebasket*: the Macintosh Recycle Bin

Using a WYSIWYG Editor

CREATING A PAGE

Textease is an example of a WYSIWYG web-authoring package.
It works in an intuitive way, as illustrated below and on pages 36
and 37. Click anywhere on a page to place an object such as text,
a graphic or a sound/video file.

Textease toolbar

The toolbar shown above contains everything you need to build a
web page template. The most frequently-used tools are shown as
icons (see page 36).

Double-clicking on an object selects it
and allows the user to drag it anywhere
on the page and drop it.

1 Using this tool
you can change
the size, shape and look of a page,
as in the example shown here, which was
set at A5 portrait with a dark background.

2 This button was
clicked to display
a *Picture Bank* from which a
background was chosen and dragged to
the title page.

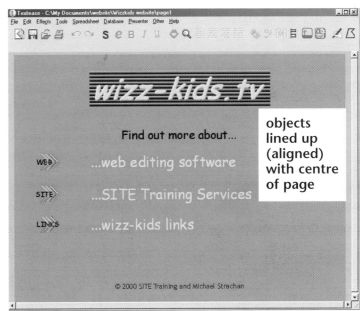

The prepared icons were inserted from their folder
into position on the template page using the *Picture
Bank* function.

3 The text subtitles were added in yellow and the
copyright warning in black.

4 The text and graphics were aligned with each
other using this set of tools from the main
menu.

This *Layouts* feature shows an array of buttons each of which
allows a different alignment of selected objects.

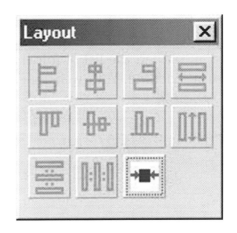

WYSIWYG editor tools and resources

Looks – change the shape, size and background colour.

Add Effects – change size, colour of text, and frames and shadow.

Picture Bank – drag and drop any picture from any folder on system.

Drawing tools

Layout

Resource Bank – drag and drop any picture or text.

horse
ladybird
ostrich
penguin
shark
starling
stickleback

beetle
common frog
cod
cuckoo
elephant
grasshopper
grass snake

Text alignment

Changes to describe each tool function briefly.

Links – create hyperlinks.

Print

This is the information line.

Save – through the filing system.

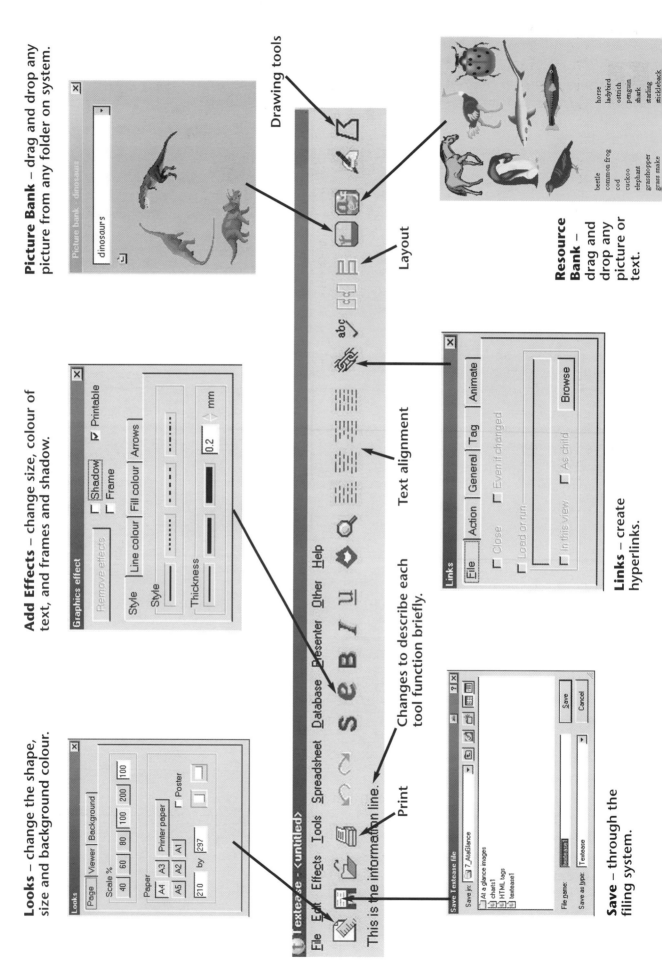

36

LINKING PAGES

With a single click, the *Links* tool can be used to link two web pages on your site.

1 On the first page, select a block of text or a graphic: red dotted lines appear round the selected item.

2 Clicking on the *Links* tool brings up a window. Click on the *Browse* button then select the page you want to link to. Its name will appear in the *Links* window.

In the example above, the silver chevron was selected and the *Browse* button was used to find the page to link to – 'page1' – and that name appeared in the window box. Objects can also be linked to other web sites by inserting a web address in the space provided instead of using the *Browse* function.

SAVING PAGES AND LINKS

When the Index page shown above is saved as a file, the link is saved, too. All other page links are created like this and tested out.

1 Save each file by first opening the *Save as* option.

2 Change the file type to HTML so that each page is saved as a web page.

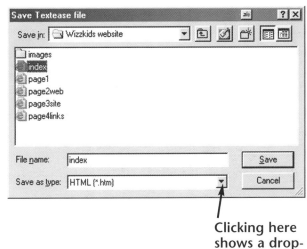

A folder named *Images* is created to contain all the pictures on every page.

To add extra pages or adapt an existing page, create it as shown above and change the destination of the linking text or graphic.

Clicking here shows a drop-down menu giving the file type options.

Using a Template Editor

The example used here is *Microsoft Publisher 2000*, which is typical among web-authoring packages that use templates.

1 Load the software in the usual way and make sure the *Publications by Wizard* tab is showing.

2 Click *Web Sites* from the list of *Wizards*.

3 Click *Start Wizard* and read the introduction.

4 After you have read the introduction click the *Next* button.

5 You will now be taken through the web page wizard, screen by screen. At each stage, you will be asked to make choices. For example, you will be asked to choose a colour scheme by highlighting and clicking from a display like this.

6 You will be asked to choose some features for your web site by clicking in boxes or 'radio buttons' like these.

7 As your web site builds you'll see it displayed in the main window.

8 You can view any of your previous pages by clicking here at the bottom of the window.

9 You can go back at any stage and change your design by clicking on a page tab at the bottom of the window.

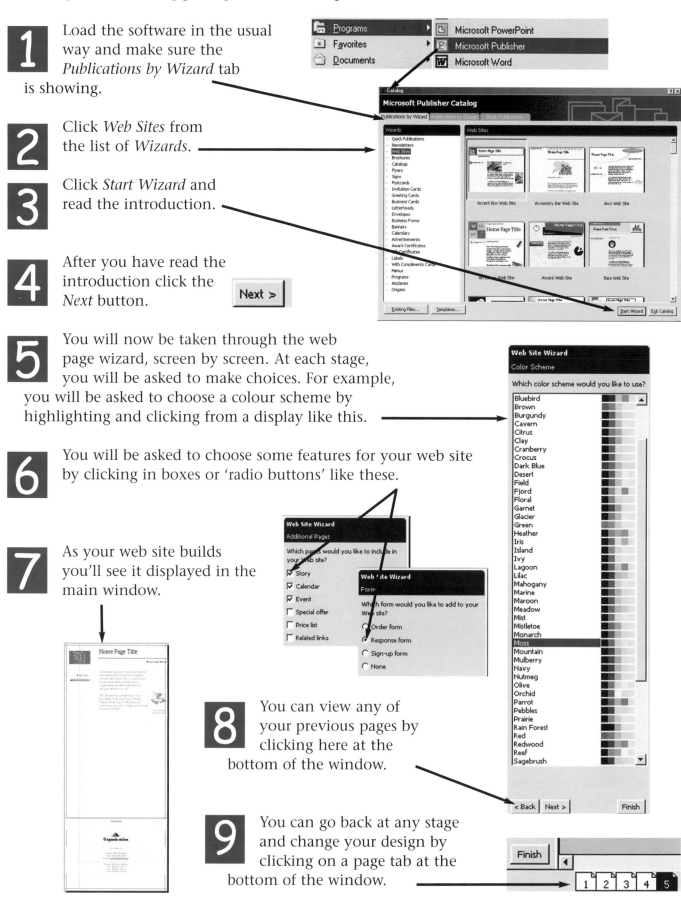

ADDING PAGES

As you follow this Wizard, you will be shown these options for adding new pages. Click in the appropriate boxes to insert the pre-designed pages you want.

If you are more confident in using *Publisher*, you may want to use the *Blank Publications* facility in creating your web pages.

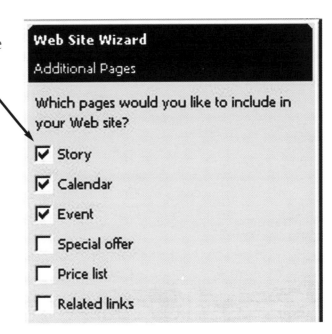

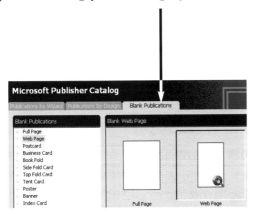

1 Use the 'page navigation control' at the bottom of the *Publisher* window to turn to where you want to insert the new page.

2 On the *Insert* menu, click *Page*.

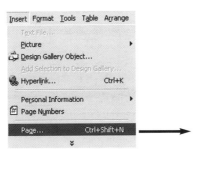

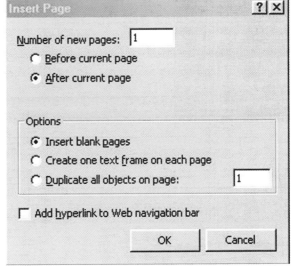

3 In the dialog box shown here, choose the options you want.

4 Confirm the changes by clicking *OK*.

Using Markup Editors

This kind of editor or web-authoring program works by displaying the 'raw' HTML. *Notepad* sets it out in plain black and white while *CuteHTML* sets it out in different colours and allows you to insert 'tags' and set up links to other pages or web sites.

Here's some of the raw HTML for the Index page of www.wizz-kids.tv produced originally in *Textease* and transferred into *CuteHTML* for checking and final editing.

```
<html>
```

```
<!-- HTML Produced by Multimedia DTP WordProcessor -->
<!--                                 -->
<!-- TextEase (R) See: http://www.textease.com     -->
<!--                                 -->
<!-- Softease Limited, England                -->
<!--                                 -->
<!-- Source file index.htm             -->
<!-- This page generated on 9th October 2001     -->
```

The image which was 'tiled' to form the page background.

```
<body bgcolor=808080 background="images\pat17.jpg"
marginheight=0 marginwidth=0 leftmargin=0
topmargin=0 rightmargin=0>
<table border=0 cellspacing=0 cellpadding=0>
<tr>
<td width=47 height=22> </td>
<td width=51 height=22> </td>
<td width=67 height=22> </td>
<td width=39 height=22> </td>
<td width=22 height=22> </td>
<td width=325 height=22> </td>
<td width=38 height=22> </td>
<td width=187 height=22> </td>
</tr>
<tr>
<td width=69 height=80> </td>
<td width=117 height=80 colspan=2> </td>
<td valign=top width=422 height=80 border=0 colspan=4>
```

This text appears in blue on the screen

```
<img src="images\clipbo.gif" border=0 >
```

```
</td>
</tr>
<tr>
<td width=69 height=102> </td>
</tr>
<tr>
<td width=69 height=10> </td>
<td width=156 height=10 colspan=3> </td>
<td valign=top width=346 height=71 border=0 rowspan=3 colspan=2>
```

This text appears in blue on the screen

```
<img src="images\_inde1.gif" border=0 >
```

The HTML tags surrounding this image made it into a button leading from the Index page to page 1.

```
</td>
</tr>
<tr>
<td width=69 height=51> </td>
<td valign=top width=51 height=51 border=0><a href="page1.htm">
```

This text appears in blue on the screen

```
<img src="images\silver.gif" HEIGHT=51 WIDTH=51 border=0 ></a>
```

```
</td>
```

HTML Tags

Here are some of the basic tags plus a few goodies which will make your pages look smart. These tags work on anything they enclose.

WHAT YOU DON'T SEE

<html></html>	Creates an HTML web page
<head></head>	Where the title and other information that isn't displayed on the web page itself are placed

WHAT YOU SEE

<body></body>	This is the visible portion of the document

HEADER TAG

<title></title>	Puts the name of the web page in the title bar

ADDING SOME COLOUR

<body bgcolor=?>	Sets the background colour
<body text=?>	Sets the text colour
<body link=?>	Sets the colour of links

PLAYING WITH THE TEXT

<b></b>	Creates bold text
<i></i>	Creates italic text
<font size=?></font>	Sets size of font
<font color=?></font>	Sets font colour

ADDING THE LINKS

<a href="URL"></a>	Creates a hyperlink to a web site address
<a href="mailto:E-MAIL"></a>	Creates a link to an e-mail program
<a name="NAME"></a>	Creates a target location within your web page
<a href="#NAME"></a>	Links to that target location from elsewhere in the web page

PUTTING IN SOME SPACE

<p></p>	Creates a new paragraph
<p align=?>	Aligns a paragraph to the left, right, or centre
 	Inserts a line break

ADDING AN IMAGE

img src="name">	Adds an image
<img src="name" align=?>	Aligns an image
<hr>	Inserts a horizontal rule

HINTS AND TIPS

These tags appear at the top of the HTML page and you can only see them in *Notepad* or a web-authoring package.

Tags must always be enclosed in their special brackets < >

? is where you type in the colour name or a special number code such as 'Black' /000000

'Teal' /008080

'Blue' /0000FF

The 'slash' is important because it turns off the tag.

HTML has set text sizes 1–7 where 7 is the largest.

A 'hyperlink' is another name for a clickable 'hot spot'.

The 'mailto' tag is the one often seen on web sites so that you can e-mail the web author.

It calls up whatever e-mail program you have set on your network or stand-alone.

Insert the alignment position at ?

 does not have to be turned off – it only creates a one line break.

You can insert left, right, centre, bottom, top, middle at ? to align an image.

41

Using a Block Editor

Programs such as *HotDog PageWiz* utilise blocks of text and graphics.

Load *PageWiz* from the *Start-Programs* route or from wherever it is on your network.

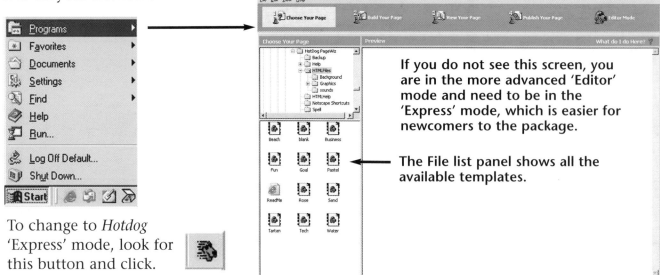

If you do not see this screen, you are in the more advanced 'Editor' mode and need to be in the 'Express' mode, which is easier for newcomers to the package.

The File list panel shows all the available templates.

To change to *Hotdog* 'Express' mode, look for this button and click.

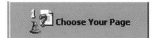

You have three choices.
You can:
1 Open a web page created in another web-authoring program.
2 Open the blank template 'blank.pwt' and create a web page from scratch.
3 Open one of the ten web page templates.

TECHNICAL TIP

Make sure you have a folder ready on your hard disk or server where you can save pages produced in *HotDog PageWiz*.

Click here to build a web page.
Topics include:

1 Adding a title
2 Headings
3 Text formatting and indenting
4 Inserting horizontal lines and images
5 Inserting animated images
6 Inserting images as links
7 Adding e-mail links.

By clicking to move to this view you can see how your page would look on the Internet and test all the links.

At this stage you can choose where your web pages will be published with all the images and links you have set up.

Clicking this button takes you to the Editor mode, which is more advanced.

Uploading the Site

To upload your web site, you need to be able to transfer all the files and images on to the server run by the company or organisation hosting your web site. This company is your Internet Service Provider and they will inform you what steps to follow to upload successfully.

Another speedy way to upload is to use a method called File Transfer Protocol, or FTP for short. There are many FTP Client packages around. The one illustrated here links with *CuteHTML* and is called *CuteFTP*.

Before you use this FTP Client program you must connect to the Internet and enter the details in a window like this. ──────→

1 Obtain your web site URL from your ISP or a commercial host company and place it in the correct window.

2 You will be supplied with a 'Username' and a 'Password', which you should store carefully and insert here.

Label for site:
wizz-kidstv

FTP Host Address:
www.wizz-kids.tv

FTP site User Name:

FTP site Password:
xxxxxxxx

FTP site connection port:
21

Login type
○ Normal
○ Anonymous
○ Double

3 To transfer files, select and highlight them in the left-hand panel using your mouse and click the upload button.

This panel shows the status of your uploads.

This panel shows the files and image folder of your web site on your school computer.

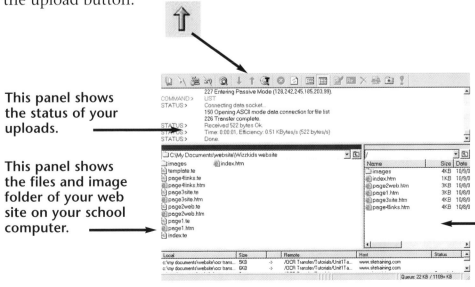

This panel shows your files and image folder transferred to the computer storing your web site.

SECTION 3:
QUESTIONS AND ANSWERS

Q HOW EASY IS IT TO SET UP A SCHOOL WEB SITE?

A Not particularly difficult, but it does require a good deal of planning, setting up and maintaining. If your school is using a software suite, such as *Textease*, which enables multimedia activities like electronic books to be made, then the natural progression is to go on and make an internal web site. This can then be used as a test bed before going online.

Q WHO IS RESPONSIBLE FOR SETTING UP THE SITE?

A This has to be agreed within the school with the headteacher and governors. The ICT co-ordinator is often given the task of building and maintaining the site, but it can be the role of any computer-literate teacher. The teacher should seek the help of other members of staff and representative parents and pupils.

Q SHOULD THERE BE A SCHOOL POLICY ABOUT MANAGING THE WEB SITE?

A Yes – this is absolutely essential. All the issues raised about content, style, management, updating and so on, should be discussed and be written into the school's policy and planning documents.

Q HOW SECURE IS THE WEB SITE?

A If you take care not to disclose the confidential information needed to upload your site then, in theory, only you and your staff and pupils can change the content and layout. Be sure that if you include personal details of staff and pupils on the site, this is on web pages that have restricted access.

Q WHAT COPYRIGHT ISSUES NEED TO BE CONSIDERED?

A Information in the form of text, data, pictures, music and video files belongs to the individual who created them, or to the group, company or organisation in which they were created. It is their 'intellectual property' and as such is protected by strict copyright laws.

You can copy/save anything from the Internet for your own personal use. But if you want to publish it in your school or personal web site, you must seek written permission from the copyright owner.

Q CAN PUPILS DAMAGE THE WEB SITE?

A It is possible, with the right level of skill, to hack into any part of the Internet, or a network. However, under the watchful eyes of teachers at school and parents at home, children are not likely to break Internet security systems. What pupils *can* easily do, however, is:

- change the start-up appearance of the desktop
- download dangerous files
- overwork/confuse the browser software.

Usually, if aspects of the desktop have been changed (such as the position of the task bar or *Start* button), the original configuration can be restored without too much trouble.

But downloading software can be dangerous. It is possible to add an application to your computer that conflicts with something already on your system. Stick to guaranteed sites and companies when hunting down new software, or install only from CD-ROMs, and you should be safe. Your ICT co-ordinator may also have her/his own policy on downloading software which is: don't do it!

If you have an Internet policy in place within the school and if parents use a filtered system and occasionally monitor what children are using and how often, then you are taking reasonable precautions.

In Section 5 of the book, Recommended Web Sites, we have provided some links to LEAs and agencies who provide specimen policies that schools can use and develop for their own needs.

Q IS AN INTERNET CONNECTION NEEDED TO MAKE AND VIEW THE WEB SITE?

A Not to make separate web pages or link them. Most of the work in designing and testing a web site can be done offline. What you end up with is an 'Intranet' – a set of linked pages that display only on your stand-alone or network computers. Creating an Intranet offers a chance to test all the effects and get the editing and management right.

Q ONCE COMPLETED, HOW CAN I UPLOAD THE WEB SITE TO THE INTERNET?

A You will need File Transfer Protocol (FTP) software to move your web site files from your school computer to its ISP. To upload your site to the ISP's server, your computer must be linked up to the Internet and online. First, you will need to insert information about your web site URL and your account details.

HINTS AND TIPS

It is advisable, particularly in school, to link up to an Internet Access Provider who has already looked at ways of preventing children accessing unsuitable sites and influences.

Generally speaking, this involves blocking or filtering certain keywords. It guarantees some peace of mind but it is not infallible. Parents and teachers need to be on guard and monitor the parts of the Internet that children visit.

Do not give out any personal, private or financial information unless you are guaranteed security by the organisation you have contacted.

Whatever system is used to create passwords, it should be consistent.

HINTS AND TIPS

Many LEAs are starting to set up local networks, or grids, to help schools establish a presence on the Internet without having to resort to special FTP software. These grids act as 'portals' – gateways to the Internet, with their own tools for web-building, and space for schools and individual teachers to have their own web sites.

Q CAN THE WEB SITE BE ALTERED ONCE IT HAS BEEN UPLOADED?

A Yes. You will need to load your FTP software, enter your username and password, then transfer new or altered pages. The software will guide you through the sequence. You can modify or update your site as many times as you wish.

Q WHAT CAN I DO WHEN THE EQUIPMENT FAILS?

A Computers sometimes 'freeze' or 'crash'. The more up-to-date your operating system, the less likely this is to happen. Holding down the CONTROL and ALT keys and pressing the DELETE key will usually identify the fault and the system may provide advice on what to do next.

If nothing appears to work, consult your manual about using the re-set button. This is a small button, usually concealed in a recess, that closes down and restarts your computer. When the computer starts up, you will almost certainly see a blue warning screen with a message about checking your hard disk for errors. The message usually clears without any further problem. If you are using a network and everything seizes up, make the ICT co-ordinator or network manager aware, but don't restart or switch off the computer. Leave it so the manager can read any warning message that has appeared on screen.

Q WHAT CAN I DO ABOUT SOFTWARE PROBLEMS AND VIRUSES?

A Many unexpected software problems that produce strange 'error messages' on screen can be sorted out by closing down your machine and restarting it. If possible, log off the network or shut down your machine in the proper way.

Viruses can find their way into your hard drive and corrupt your software or operating software. One precaution against viruses is to avoid, or restrict the use of, floppy disks. Many schools now do this. Ensure your system is equipped with an up-to-date virus checker for examining disks and files.

Q HOW CAN I AVOID LOSING AN INTERNET CONNECTION?

A Browsers such as *Internet Explorer* and *Netscape Navigator* are complex pieces of software and prone to unexpected glitches. Keep track of where you are, for example by bookmarking sites or jotting down URLs, so that you can get back to a site easily after a crash. Sometimes a lost connection can be sorted out by pressing the REFRESH button at the top of the screen page.

HINTS AND TIPS

To identify any fault, start at the most basic possible source of trouble, such as power supply, plugs and fuses, loose connections.

If you come back to a computer that has been in use and the screen is blank, it may just be that it is in power-saving mode. Jiggle the mouse and the screen may reappear.

If a printer stops working, check that the ink cartridges or toner cartridge are not empty and that there is sufficient dry, clean, uncreased paper in the feeder.

Never close down a machine by turning off the power or unplugging it from the mains.

HINTS AND TIPS

Go online regularly to update your virus-checking software.

HINTS AND TIPS

Where possible, stagger Internet access to avoid large groups trying to access the same site at the same time.

If the problem continues and access is denied, or is very slow, have some alternative classroom activities available.

SECTION 4: **Photocopiable Projects**

Teachers' notes

The following photocopiable activities are designed to help children practise ICT skills in topic work across the curriculum. The projects provide opportunities for children to create, develop and design web pages on a wide range of themes. They link with literacy work by encouraging children to write for a purpose and consider their audience. The activity sheets provide frameworks by which the children can plan web pages on paper and research any necessary information before moving on to the computer. The activity sheets are also valuable assessment tools.

Most of the projects can be completed by children working in groups. The activities generally contain an off-screen element where the children work on paper, followed by an on-screen activity. Children are encouraged to use a range of resources for research, including the Internet.

 The icon shown here indicates any parts of the activity sheets that need to be completed online.

It is not expected that the activities will be completed in one lesson, and at the end of each sheet there is a suggestion for a **Next step**, or a way of extending the project. Many of the suggestions involve using the ideas on the sheet to create a web page at the computer, which may be completed over a number of lessons.

The following notes provide suggestions for ways of making the most of the activities and introducing, adapting or extending them.

What are web sites for? (page 52)
This activity encourages children to think about the audience and purpose of school web sites. You could mask the web site URLs and insert ones for schools in your area or for school web sites you have visited. For the Next step, encourage the children to think about how they will frame the questions, for example, as open questions or as multiple choice. The information could be shared among the whole class and collated in a chart.

For and against a web site (page 53)
Begin by discussing the kinds of information that you could put on a school web site and encourage the children to think about what possible advantages and disadvantages there might be. They might think about the practical aspects of creating a web site, for example, how it will help their ICT skills. Or they might think about what benefits can be had from displaying their work on a web site and publicising school events. They could also think about the impression that visitors to the web site will form of the school if the site and hyperlinks are not updated regularly.

Web site questionnaire (page 54)
Arrange for the children to e-mail their questionnaires to pupils at another primary or secondary school who have been involved in setting up and maintaining a school web site. When the children receive replies, encourage them to use the information to generate original ideas and to think of ways to overcome any potential problems.

What goes on a web site? (page 55)
The children can complete this activity in pairs or groups. They should think about the audience of the web site and what information will be most useful to them. Encourage children to give reasons for their ordering of the cards. During follow-up discussion, ask the children which cards they discarded and why. Discuss why it is important not to publish personal details such as pupils' names and addresses. As an extension activity, these cards could be used to make a spidergram (see Spidergram links, page 57).

Using hyperlinks (page 56)
Give the children opportunities to use hyperlinks on existing web sites and ensure that they understand the concept of hyperlinks. The underlining activity could be repeated using the children's own written compositions. For the Next step, each child or group could choose one sport, for which they write text and create an icon using a drawing program. The pages can then be linked to a home page giving an introduction to sports facilities at the school.

Spidergram links (page 57)
For this activity, children may think of different ways the web pages could be linked, for example, the interview with Forrest Wilson could link to Humorous books or to your class's favourite authors. It could link to both of these pages.

Web site review (page 58)
You could mask the web site URLs and insert ones for schools in your area or for school web sites you have visited. When the children have completed the chart, they could compare their notes with a friend, and discuss what makes a good home page, what makes a web page clear and easy to read (thinking about the use of colour, sub-headings and paragraphs) and so on. They could also think about other features of web sites, such as whether pages take a long time to download and the use of counters to say how many people have visited the web site.

Plan your school web site (page 59)
The children should first complete the spidergram activity on page 57. Before beginning the activity, discuss what information could go on a school web site. The cards on page 55 may be useful as starting points. The text on this page could be masked to provide a template for planning any set of hyperlinks.

Plan a home page (page 60)
The children should first complete Plan your school web site (page 59). Allow the children to visit home pages of other school web sites to help them gather ideas for features to include. Discuss

with the children why it is important to have an exciting and easy-to-use home page.

Home page pictures (page 61)
Use this activity as a follow-up to Plan a home page (page 60). Encourage the children to think of pictures that represent opening or entering in some way. The messages on the pictures should be lively and snappy. The children can create a home page on the computer using their favourite idea.

Counting visitors (page 62)
Ask the children to share their suggestions for ways to increase the number of hits on the school web site. Discuss reasons why the number of hits might increase or decrease over certain time periods, including external factors such as holidays.

Changing text: 1 (page 63)
Introduce the activity by showing the children texts with different styles of headings and sub-headings. Discuss that a main heading appears in large bold type, and may be centred or written in capital letters. Sub-headings are written in smaller type than the main heading, but larger than the body text. Explain that a wavy underline is the proof correction mark for bold text. To provide further practice in writing headings and sub-headings, you could cut off the headlines from short newspaper reports, then give them to the children and ask them to think of suitable headlines. For the Next step, you may wish to which ties in with topic work in other areas of the Curriculum.

Changing text: 2 (page 64)
Use this activity in conjunction with Changing text: 1 (page 63). It will also be helpful if the children have first completed Using hyperlinks (page 56). For the Next step, explain that glossary words on a web page can be hyperlinked to a glossary page.

Colours and backgrounds (page 65)
To introduce the activity, you could let the children experiment with text colours by writing words (such as the names of fruit) in different colours on white or coloured paper. Display the results and discuss with the children which ones are easiest to read, and why. You could also show the children a photo of a rainbow and explain that colours on opposite sides of the rainbow go well together. For the Next step, the children can choose a background for a web page they have created in another activity, or for any piece of text they have written for the school web site.

A book review template (page 66)
Explain to the children that when you fill in a template, you save it under a new name, so the template itself remains blank and can be used again and again. You could ask different groups of children to make different kinds of templates, for example, for film reviews or music reviews. An e-mail link could be added to the web site so that visitors to the site can contribute their opinions on the books reviewed.

A tour of our school (page 67)
To introduce the concept of using hyperlinks to 'zoom in' on a map or plan, the children could visit www.multimap.com, where they can click on a part of the map to see a more detailed map of that area. The children could complete this activity in small groups. You could allocate a part of the school to each group so that between them they will plan out the entire school, including the grounds. The plans can then be put together on the computer (a separate plan will be needed for each storey of the school). Provide squared paper for children who require more space for drawing their plans. The rooms need not be drawn to scale. Encourage the children to think about what information will be of interest to parents visiting the web site, such as which facilities are in which room. Photographs of some of the rooms could be scanned in and displayed on the web pages.

A photo gallery (page 68)
The children could visit web sites of other schools and look at the photographs on display. They could make notes about what each photograph tells them and what impression it gives of the school (for example, friendly, hard-working, welcoming, multi-cultural and so on). If possible, allow the children to take a limited number of photographs based on their ideas and scan them in. These could be used in a photograph gallery on the school web site.

Our school history (page 69)
To introduce the activity, ask the children what they already know about the school's history. If possible, provide old school newsletters, newspaper clippings and photographs for them to use in their research. The children could interview a former pupil or someone who has worked at the school for a long time. They could include quotes or a transcript of the interview on the web page.

Our school day (page 70)
The children may wish to choose significant times of the day, such as assembly, break time, lunchtime and home time. Alternatively, the children could work in a group and between them cover all the events of the school day. To illustrate their web pages, children can add photographs of school activities, draw and scan in their own illustrations, or use copyright-free clip art from CD-ROMs or the Internet.

A class diary (page 71)
If you wish, you could ask the children to write about things they have done over the past week or past term, by masking and altering the first instruction. Suitable activities include days out, class assemblies, fundraising events and so on; a list could be drawn up in a brainstorming session as an introduction to the activity.

A school trip (page 72)
This activity makes an ideal follow-up to a class outing. If any photographs were taken on the outing, allow the children to write captions for them and choose which ones they would like to put on the web page. Provide blank pieces of paper on which the children can write any further details they wish. Encourage them to put the pieces of paper in a logical order for their recount and include arrows to show hyperlinks to other web pages (hyperlinks could include links to the official web site of the place visited and to relevant history web sites).

A music web page (page 73)
To introduce the activity, ask the children to think about who might be interested in a web page about the school's music activities, for example, parents or new pupils. The initial data-collecting exercise could be done as a whole-class activity.

Star pupils (page 74)
Before beginning the activity, discuss what sort of achievements children can be proud of: anything from a good piece of work to giving up time to help family, friends or neighbours. The activity will help children to evaluate their own achievements and those of their classmates, and also to think about the value of working co-operatively in a group.

A web invitation (page 75)
Use this activity when a school event is approaching, such as sports day, fundraising events or celebrations. Alternatively, the children could imagine an event that might take place and make up the details. Ask the children to discuss the advantages and disadvantages of advertising an event on a web site.

Start a collection (page 76)
With the class, decide what you want to start collecting, for example, book tokens, money, food or clothes for charity, or bric-a-brac for a jumble sale. Decide together how the collection will be organised and where people should take donations. Encourage the children to use persuasive language and catchy slogans in their advertisement to capture the readers' interest.

A review of resources (page 77)
Before photocopying the sheet, you could write on a topic that the children are studying, for example, the Tudors, the Solar System or festivals. The children can search for web sites, using search engines (such as www.KidsClick.com or www.askco.uk), or you could write suitable web site URLs on the sheet first. For help with finding web sites, refer to the *Finding Information* title in this series. Try to provide a range of different web sites so that the children are not all reviewing the same ones, although some overlap is recommended to allow the children to compare opinions. The children will also need access to

relevant books and CD-ROMs. When compiling their information, they may find it helpful to cut out the boxes on the chart.

Welcoming visitors (page 78)
Invite children who know how to say or write greetings in languages other than English to share their knowledge with the class. Provide foreign-language pocket dictionaries or allow the children to log on to the Fodor's web site, where they can learn French, German, Italian or Spanish and can also hear the words spoken. The children will also need reference books which show countries' flags.

A local building (page 79)
Provide a selection of books, magazines and leaflets about the local area to help the children choose a building. Encourage children to find information on the Internet by using a search engine or by visiting tourist information or local council web sites. They should make a note of any particularly useful web site URLs and use them as hyperlinks for their own web pages.

Go green! (page 80)
To introduce the topic, ask the children what they already know about car pollution. You could show the children examples of leaflets aimed at encouraging people to use cars less often. The chart can be filled in as a whole-class activity. When the children write their arguments, encourage them to think about the disadvantages of using public transport or bicycles and to offer ideas for how these problems can be overcome.

The mystery door (page 81)
Before beginning the activity, the class could brainstorm story genres such as historical fiction, fantasy, romance, mystery and so on. Encourage them to choose a particular genre for their story. Once the children have written their stories, encourage them to edit and refine the story before reaching the final version.

Science quiz (page 82)
You could enter a science topic that the children are studying on the sheet before photocopying. Ensure that the children check the accuracy of their facts in a reference book. Some children could give visual clues instead of written statements, for example, labelled diagrams, which may be either correct or incorrect.

Make a fun web page (page 83)
Encourage the children to incorporate any other fun ideas they can think of. You could use this activity to link with topic work across the Curriculum, for example, by asking the children to make quizzes, crosswords or wordsearches on a particular theme. Word puzzles could be made to tie in with word-level work that is being studied. For the Next step, the children could record their own laughter or they could go to web site www.vionline.com/sound.html to find a sound file.

What are web sites for?

Go to one of these school web sites.

Circle the one you choose.

www.kelsall.school.cheshire.org.uk

www.aldboroughprimary.norfolk.sch.uk

List three things that you can do or find out about at the web site.

I. _____

2. _____

3. _____

Who do you think the web site is aimed at? _____

_____

Why do you think this? _____

_____

_____

Think about how you could make a great web site for your school. Write three things you would put on it.

Idea bank

I. _____

_____

2. _____

_____

3. _____

_____

Next step
- Ask a parent, a teacher and a friend what they would find useful or interesting on a school web site and why.
- Write or word-process the information as a report to the headteacher.

Check your spelling.

For and against a web site

Look at what these people say about creating a web site. Which are arguments for a web site and which are arguments against? Write 'For' or 'Against' next to each person.

Parents and pupils visit the web site regularly. They are more involved with school activities.

My web site cost a lot of money to set up.

Creating web pages is fun!

I think people should use public transport more often. My web site helps me get this message across.

We have to spend a lot of time keeping the information on the web site up to date.

We raised money for the NSPCC on our web site.

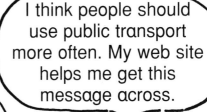

Can you think of more advantages or disadvantages of creating and looking after a web site? Write them in the bubbles.

Next step
- Make a list of information on your school web site that you would need to update regularly.
- For each one, write how often you think you would need to update it.

Internet Projects for Primary Schools
Creating a Web Site
© A & C Black 2002

Web site questionnaire

You are going to write a questionnaire to send to a school that has set up a web site. Use the questionnaire to find out how successful their web site is.

Write a list of questions or instructions for your questionnaire.

You might want to ask:

- why the school set up the web site

- what the advantages and disadvantages are

- what things are/have been on the web site

- what helpful hints do they have for building a school web site.

Think of other things you would like to ask. Don't forget to find out the web site URL!

Write your questions in an e-mail.

 Send your e-mail to that school.

Check your spelling.

Next step

- When you receive a reply from the school, write a report about how useful the information is. Include your own ideas for creating and running your school web site.

Internet Projects for Primary Schools
Creating a Web Site
© A & C Black 2002

What goes on a web site?

Each card on this page shows information you can include on your school web site. Cut out the cards and put them in order of importance. Start with the most important. Put aside cards you do not wish to use.

Work with a friend

Where to buy school uniform	Date of the next parents' evening
School rules	Name of the headteacher
How many pupils the school has 	Information about sports day
Information on music lessons	Picture of your class 
E-mail address to contact for more information	What football team your best friend supports 
Name of the PE teacher	Name of the school
What your teacher had for breakfast this morning	Details of Class 6E's recycling project
How old the school is	School telephone number
Names and addresses of all the pupils who attend the school	Picture of the school grounds 
How to find the school	

Next step
- Compare your ordering of the cards with another group's.
- Discuss why you chose this order.

Internet Projects for Primary Schools
Creating a Web Site
© A & C Black 2002

Using hyperlinks

A hyperlink is a piece of text or a picture. You can click on it to take you to another web page.

Get <u>TV listings</u> for all your favourite programmes!

Hyperlink text is underlined.

Click on the icon to find out more about London.

Hyperlink picture, or icon.

Read the passage from a web site. <u>Underline</u> the words that you could make into hyperlinks. Using a colour pencil, draw hyperlink icons on the map.

On our class trip to <u>York</u> we visited York Minster, which has a very beautiful stained glass window called the Rose Window. In 1984, the Minster was struck by lightning and the window was damaged, but it has since been carefully restored. We also went to the Jorvik Viking Centre. Jorvik is the Viking name for York. At the Centre we found out what life was like in Britain in the tenth century. We toured the Viking city in time capsules. Afterwards we had a group photograph taken by the River Ouse.

map showing where York is and how to get there

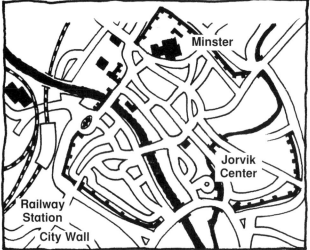

River Ouse

Draw hyperlink icons for a web page about sport. Choose pictures that link to the sports.

football		cricket		athletics	

hockey		rugby		netball	

Next step
- Look at a history book about the Vikings, then design hyperlink icons that could be used on a Vikings web site.
 ● Go to <u>iconbank.com/gx/index.htm</u>. Find an icon that you could use on a web site about music or art.

Spidergram links

You can plan hyperlinks for web pages on a spidergram, like this.

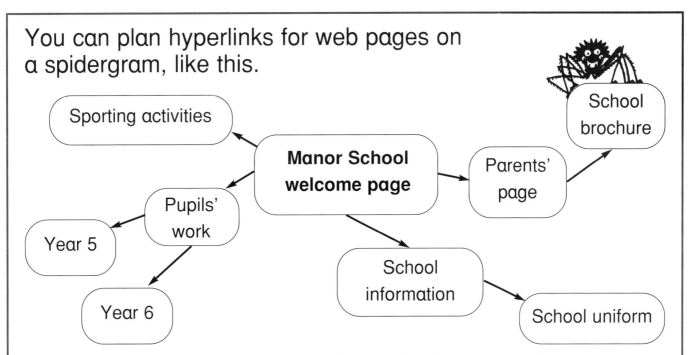

Cut out the web page titles below, which are all about books read by one class. Arrange the cards in a spidergram on a blank sheet of paper. Draw in the arrows.

Next step

● Think of other web pages you could add. Write the web page titles on extra cards and add them to the spidergram where they belong. Glue the cards in position.

57

Web site review

To help you decide how to design your school web site, it is useful to review other school web sites.

 Go to the web sites on the chart.
Make notes about the sites.

	Burbage Junior School www.burbage-jun.leics.sch.uk	Friarswood Primary School www.friarswood.org.uk
Is the home page (welcome page) helpful?		
Is it easy to find your way around the site?		
Is the information up to date?		
Do the pages look appealing?		
Do the colours make the text easy to read?		
Are there sound files, photographs and animations?		
Is it easy to find out how to contact the school?		
Have pupils created the whole site, or just some pages?		

Write a sentence to say which web site you thought was the better, and why.

Next step
- Make a list of design features you think are important for your school web site. Use the notes on the chart to help you.
- Number the features in order of importance (1 = most important).

Plan your school web site

Use this page to plan the hyperlinks for your school web site.

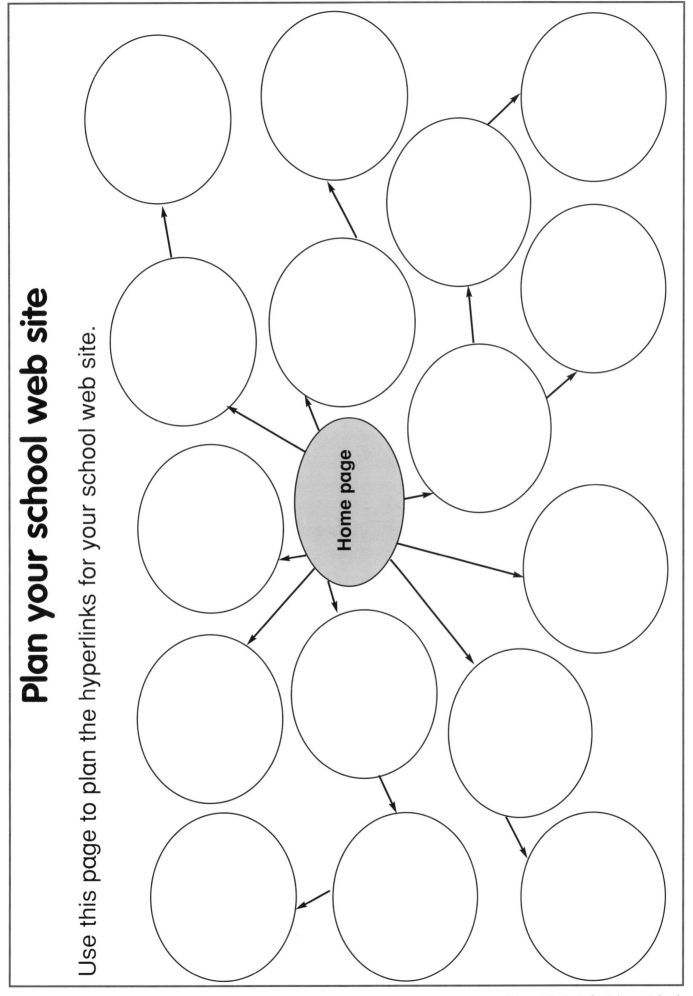

Home page

Plan a home page

A home page introduces a web site. Plan a home page for your school web site. Use your hyperlink planning sheet to help you.

Home page heading	
Introduction	
Picture	Photograph
Sound file	Animation
Hyperlink icon	Hyperlink icon
Text hyperlink	Text hyperlink
Text hyperlink	Text hyperlink

Write a paragraph about your web site. Describe the main topics. Make it sound exciting!

Draw a picture and a photograph you will include.

Describe sounds and animations (cartoons) you will use.

Design icons for hyperlinks.

Write titles of other pages on the site to make into hyperlinks.

Next step
- Cut along the dotted lines. Move the cards around to help you design your home page.
- Create your home page on the computer, using your design.

Home page pictures

A home page does not need lots of information. It can have a short message and a picture which you click on to enter the web site.

Think of different pictures that you could put on a home page of your school web site. Draw your ideas.

Write a message on each picture.

Think about how you can make the page look inviting. You could draw a building, an animal or some sort of box to open . . .

Next step
- Discuss with a friend the advantages of a simple home page for your school web site. Then discuss the advantages of a home page with lots of information. Which do you prefer, and why?

61

Counting visitors

You can put a counter on a web site. It tells you how many people have visited the site.
The number of people is called the number of 'hits'.

5	9	6	2

5,962 hits

Go to this web site: www.st-birinus.oxon.sch.uk

Find the counter on the home page. How many hits has the web site had?

_____ hits since _____

Write why you think a school might want a counter on its web site.

_____

_____

_____

Idea bank

WEBSITE OF THE YEAR

J F M A M J

Think of six ways you could increase the number of hits on your school web site.

_____

_____

_____

_____

_____

How can you make sure people visit your web site regularly?

Next step

- Go to this web site www.counter4.free.com.
- Choose a counter for your school web site. Write a sentence explaining why you chose this one.

Changing text: 1

Headings and sub-headings make a piece of text easier to read.

A main heading tells the reader what the whole text is about.

Sub-headings tell the reader what different parts of the text are about.

ART AT OUR SCHOOL

Artists studied
We are studying a group of artists known as the Impressionists. The group started in France in the 1860s. The artists focused on the changing effects of light. The Impressionists include Vincent Van Gogh, Claude Monet and Pierre-Auguste Renoir.

Visit to a museum
Years 5 and 6 have travelled to the Courtauld Gallery in London to see an exhibition of Impressionist paintings. They are now writing a report about their visit.

Read this text about the artist Vincent Van Gogh.

Vincent Van Gogh. When and where born. Van Gogh was born on 30 March 1853 in the village of Groot-Zundert in the Netherlands. Family. Van Gogh was the oldest of six children. He had three sisters and two brothers. His father was a clergyman. Education. Van Gogh went to a village school until he was 13. He went to a boarding school in 1864. Mental illness. Van Gogh became mentally ill and suffered from hallucinations and breakdowns. In 1888 he cut off part of his own ear. When died. Van Gogh shot himself on 27 July 1890. He died two days later, aged 37. Famous paintings by Van Gogh. Van Gogh's most famous painting is called 'Sunflowers'. He also painted many self-portraits. Between 1885 and 1888 he completed more than 40 pictures of himself in various moods. Museums where you can find Van Gogh's paintings. Most of Van Gogh's paintings are in a museum in Amsterdam which is especially devoted to his work. Other museums which have examples of his work include the National Gallery (London), the Museum of Modern Art (New York), the Louvre (Paris) and the Musée d'Orsay (Paris).

Underline in red the main heading. Underline in blue the sub-headings.

Bullet points make a list easier to read. Circle a part of the text that you could re-write using bullet points.

Examples of bullet points:
- Lowry
- Turner
- Monet

Next step
- Word-process a piece of text for a web page. It could be about a school event or something your class is studying. Use a main heading and sub-headings.
- Under one of the sub-headings, change the text to a list with bullet points.

Check your spelling.

Changing text: 2

This is what the Van Gogh text might look like on a web page.

Think about hyperlinks you could add. Underline the hyperlink words. Write at the side what might be on the linking page.

There might be pictures or explaining text.

VINCENT VAN GOGH

When and where born. Van Gogh was born on 30 March 1853 in the village of Groot-Zundert in the Netherlands.

map of the Netherlands showing the village

Family. Van Gogh was the oldest of six children. He had three sisters and two brothers. His father was a clergyman.

Education. Van Gogh went to a village school until he was 13. He went to a boarding school in 1864.

Mental illness. Van Gogh became mentally ill and suffered from hallucinations and breakdowns. In 1888 he cut off part of his own ear.

When died. Van Gogh shot himself on 27 July 1890. He died two days later, aged 37.

Famous paintings by Van Gogh. Van Gogh's most famous painting is called 'Sunflowers'. He also painted many self-portraits. Between 1885 and 1888 he completed more than 40 pictures of himself in various moods.

Museums where you can find Van Gogh's paintings. Most of Van Gogh's paintings are in a museum in Amsterdam which is especially devoted to his work.
Other museums which have examples of his work include:
- the National Gallery (London)
- the Museum of Modern Art (New York)
- the Louvre (Paris)
- the Musée d'Orsay (Paris).

Next step
- Use a wavy underline to mark words that you think should go in a glossary.
- Write the glossary.

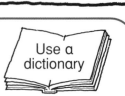

Use a dictionary

64

Colours and backgrounds

You can make a web page more interesting with coloured text and backgrounds.

Remember, your text needs to be easy to read!

In a word-processing program, write a sentence about your favourite subject.

Change the colour of the text. Then change the colour of the background. Can you still read the text?

Try these colour pairs.

Blue text on yellow background		Red text on green background		Pink text on blue background	

Which is the easiest to read? ✔ (Tick the box.)

You can also use a patterned background. This is from a web page about Christmas.

Click here for more festive fun!

Design background patterns for web pages on these subjects.

swimming	aeroplanes	insects

Next step

- Go to this web site www.free-graphics.com.
- Choose a background for a web page you have created. Copy the background on to your web page.
- Change the colour of your text. Make sure the text is easy to read.

Internet Projects for Primary Schools
Creating a Web Site
© A & C Black 2002

A book review template

You are going to make a web page template for writing book reviews. You can use the same template for several reviews.

First, look at this example template. Fill it in for a book you have read recently.

Title of book:	Author:
Genre:	Time when story is set:

Place where story is set:

Brief outline of the plot (don't give the whole story away!):

What the main characters are like:	Main themes of the book:

I do/do not recommend this book because:

Next step
- Now create a template on the computer. It could like the one above, or you could make up your own.
- Ask three friends to fill in a copy of the template for books they have read. Display them on your school web site.

Internet Projects for Primary Schools
Creating a Web Site
© A & C Black 2002

A tour of our school

You are going to make a web page which shows a plan of your school. When visitors click on a room, a hyperlink takes them to a page with more information about that room.

Example:

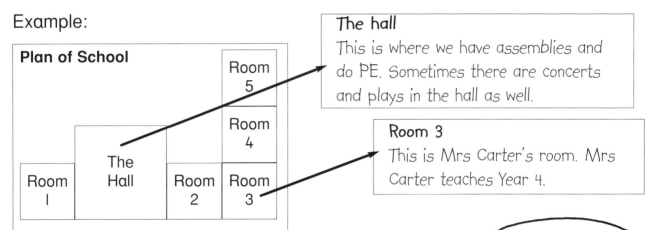

Plan of School

| Room 1 | The Hall | Room 2 | Room 3 | Room 4 | Room 5 |

The hall
This is where we have assemblies and do PE. Sometimes there are concerts and plays in the hall as well.

Room 3
This is Mrs Carter's room. Mrs Carter teaches Year 4.

Choose part of your school for your plan.
Draw your plan on the grid.
Draw and label each room.

You could choose a whole storey, or part of one.

Word-process a sentence or short paragraph about each room to explain what happens there.

Next step
- Create your plan in a drawing program.
- Add hyperlinks so that when visitors click on a room, they can read your text telling them more about the room.

Check your spelling.

A photo gallery

Photographs can tell people a lot about what your school is like.

Look at these pictures of a school. What do they tell you about this school? Write notes under the pictures.

1.  2.  3.

1. _____

2. _____

3. _____

Imagine you can take only three photos to tell people about your school. Describe each photo you would take. Think of a caption for each one.

Photo 1
Where?

_____

_____

Who/what?

_____

_____

Caption:

_____

_____

Photo 2
Where?

_____

_____

Who/what?

_____

_____

Caption:

_____

_____

Photo 3
Where?

_____

_____

Who/what?

_____

_____

Caption:

_____

_____

Next step
- With a friend, plan a photo gallery for your school web site. Think about how you can show other people things that happen at your school during the year. Draw a plan to show how you will arrange the photos. Write captions.

Our school history

Use this page to plan a web page about the history of your school. Make notes about what you will include.

Write down extra things you need to find out.

Heading _____

Introduction _____
_____
_____

Things I will write about:
_____
_____
_____
_____
_____
_____

You might want to write about:
THEN and NOW
- school uniform
- the school building
- school dinners
- the school day
- important events in the school's history
- what your school might be like in 100 years' time.

Think about photographs you could include and people you could interview.

Other things to go on the web page: _____
_____
_____

Next step
- Word-process the text for your web page. Research any extra information you need.
- Add an e-mail link so that former pupils can e-mail the school with more information.

Check your spelling.

Internet Projects for Primary Schools
Creating a Web Site
© A & C Black 2002

Our school day

You are going to create web pages showing what you do during your school day.

Choose four different times during the school day. Write them in the boxes.

Use the 24-hour clock, e.g. 09:00, 13:15.

Write what you are usually doing at that time. Describe where you are, who you are with and whether you enjoy yourself.

Use these cards to show hyperlinks between pages.

Use these cards to show the reader how to get back to the main page.

back back

back back

Now cut out the cards. Arrange them to make a plan of your web pages.

Our school day

| 09:00 |
| 12:00 |
| 10:45 |
| 13:15 |

→ **Assembly**
After registration, all children must go to the main hall for assembly. Then they must return to their classes.

← back

Next step
- Create your web pages. Include drawings, photographs or clip art. Don't forget to write a heading for each page.
- Create the hyperlinks between the pages.

Check your spelling.

70

A class diary

Think about things you have done with your class in the past month. Choose three activities.

| Date | Date | Date |
| Activity | Activity | Activity |

Write a diary entry for each date.

| November 2002 |
S	M	T	W	T	F	S
					1	2
3	4	5	6	7	8	9
10	11	12	13	14	15	16
17	18	19	20	21	22	23
24	25	26	27	28	29	30

Date

Date

Date

Describe each activity. Explain who, what, when, where, why. Make it sound exciting!

Next step
- Edit and re-draft your diary entries on a web page.
- Make the dates stand out from the rest of the text. Add pictures, bars or lines to separate the diary entries.

Check your spelling.

Internet Projects for Primary Schools
Creating a Web Site
© A & C Black 2002

A school trip

Use this page to plan a web page about a school trip you have been on.

OUR TRIP TO
EDINBURGH CASTLE
HISTORY OF THE CASTLE

We visited

on

Three things I saw/did

1	2	3

Three things I learnt

1	2	3

My favourite part of the visit

My least favourite part of the visit

Cut along the dotted lines. Rearrange the information to show how it will appear on your web page.

On separate pieces of paper you could . . .

| write headings and sub-headings | draw pictures or photographs to be included | choose hyperlinks (underline the hyperlink text) | add any more information you want |

Next step
- Write your text on a web page. Use headings and sub-headings. Add hyperlinks.

Check your spelling.

Internet Projects for Primary Schools
Creating a Web Site
© A & C Black 2002

A music web page

You are going to create a web page about music activities at your school.

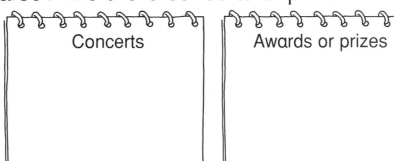

Write on the chart five instruments that children learn to play. Find out how many children in your class play each instrument.

Instrument	Number of children who play it

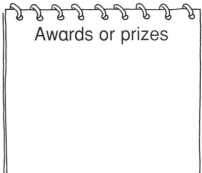

In a data-handling program, create a bar chart to show the information. Don't forget to give the bar chart a title.

Now make notes about your school orchestra, band or choir. When do pupils rehearse? Are there concerts or prizes?

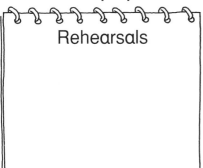

Rehearsals

Concerts

Awards or prizes

Use your notes to help you word-process a piece of text for your web page.

Check your spelling.

Next step
- Record a sound file for your web page of someone playing a musical instrument.
- Create your music web page. Draw a plan of the page on paper, then create it on the computer.

Internet Projects for Primary Schools
Creating a Web Site
© A & C Black 2002

Star pupils

You are going to make a web page to show what you and your friends have achieved this week.

Write about the school work you are most proud of.

Idea bank

_____

_____

Write about something helpful that a classmate has done for you this week.

_____

_____

Now think of something that your class or group has worked together to achieve this week.

_____

_____

Word-process a paragraph for each achievement. Say why you and your friends are proud of the achievements.

Check your spelling.

Did you have to work hard to succeed? Did you think of others before yourselves?

Using a drawing program, draw three large stars, trophies or rosettes for your web page. Think about what colours you will use. Will you include any writing?

Next step
- *Create a web page that shows the three star, trophy or rosette graphics. Remember to give the page a title.*
- *Create hyperlinks so that when someone clicks on a graphic, they can read about one of the achievements.*

Internet Projects for Primary Schools
Creating a Web Site
© A & C Black 2002

A web invitation

A web site that is visited by lots of people is an ideal place to display invitations to special events.

Think of an event that is going to take place at your school.

Please come to our
Summer Fair

Saturday 14 June
2 p.m. – 7 p.m.
Dotheboy's Hall

Tombola • Music • Big Prizes • Raffles

Event _____

Make notes about the information you will include on the invitation.

Date	Time (start and finish)	Place

Entry price adults children	Special attractions	Other reasons why people should come

| E-mail address to contact for more information | | |

Draw a plan of your invitation on paper. Think of pictures or animations you could use.

Next step
- Create your invitation on a web page. Think about how you will design the page, how you will vary the size of the text and what colours you will use.

Check your spelling.

Internet Projects for Primary Schools
Creating a Web Site
© A & C Black 2002

Start a collection

With your class, decide on something to start collecting. Write an advertisement for your web site to persuade people to help you with your collection.

Think of a catchy heading for your advertisement.

Say what you are collecting and why.

Make up a slogan that uses alliteration (e.g. We need tons of tokens!)

Draw an entertaining picture.

Say what your target number is. Make the readers feel like they can realistically help you reach it.

Tell readers where to take donations and what to do if they want more information.

Next step
- Create your advertisement on a web page.
- Design a thank you certificate to give to people who help you with your collection.

Internet Projects for Primary Schools
Creating a Web Site
© A & C Black 2002

A review of resources

You are going to find resources (such as books, web sites and CD-ROMs) on a subject and review them for your school web site.

Choose a topic you are studying at school.

Topic _____

Find the URLs of three web sites on this subject. Write them on the chart.

Go to each web site. Make notes on the chart about the information you find and how useful it is.

Find books and CD-ROMs on the subject. Make notes about these as well.

Web site URL/ book/CD-ROM	Notes (what information/how useful)

In your group, decide which web sites, books and CD-ROMs are the most useful. Give reasons why. Compile your notes on these resources for a web page.

Next step
- *Create the web page. It might look something like this:*
- *Hyperlink the web site URLs so that visitors can click on them to go to the web sites.*

Class 4C's review of resources
Resource   What we think

Internet Projects for Primary Schools
Creating a Web Site
© A & C Black 2002

Welcoming visitors

Use this page to plan a web page to greet foreign visitors.

Choose a greeting word, such as 'welcome' or 'hello'. Find out how to write it in five different languages. Fill in the chart.

Find a picture of the country's flag. Draw it on the chart.

Bienvenue!

Guten Tag!

Use dictionaries or go to www.fodors.com/language/

Language	Greeting word	Country where spoken	Flag

Create your web page. Write a title and an introduction. Display the greeting words and the flags. Scan in pictures of the flags or create them in a drawing program.

Welcome!

Willkomen!

Next step
- Find out how to say the greetings. Record them using a sound recording program.
- Create hyperlinks so that when someone clicks on the greeting word, they hear the greeting spoken.

78

A local building

Create a web page discussing an interesting building in your local area.
First, choose a building.

Building   Why I have chosen it

Use books, leaflets and the Internet to find out more about the building. Plan your web page using the cards.

> Make a note of the URL where you found the information.

Web page heading	When building was built
Who built it and why?	What happens there today?
Other interesting information	

Picture	Picture
Hyperlink icon	Hyperlink icon
Hyperlink	Hyperlink

Draw or describe pictures and icons.

Write URLs to hyperlink to your web page.

Next step
- Cut along the dotted lines. Move the cards around to help you design your web page.
- Create your web page. Add an e-mail link so that people can contact you with extra interesting facts they know about the building.

Internet Projects for Primary Schools
Creating a Web Site
© A & C Black 2002

Go green!

You are going to create a web page encouraging people to use their cars less often.

Ask your classmates how they travel to school. Fill in the tally chart. Use the data to create a pie chart. Give the pie chart a title.

Now list the advantages and disadvantages of travelling by car.

Way of travelling	Tally	Total
Car	~~HHT~~	
Train		
Bicycle		
On foot		
Other		

Advantages	Disadvantages

Idea bank

Use persuasive language. Appeal to the reader's point of view.

Word-process a piece of writing for your web page that explains the disadvantages of travelling by car. Write a heading, an introduction and a conclusion.

Check your spelling.

Next step
- Copy your text on to a web page. Add the pie chart you created.
- Find web sites that give information about public transport and cycle lanes in your area. Hyperlink these sites to your web page.

The mystery door

Use this page to plan a story about a character (or characters) who goes through a mystery door. Use the pictures to help you think of ideas.

Who are the main characters? Describe them.

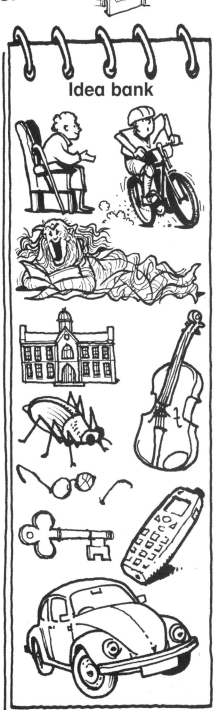

Idea bank

Where is the door? How do the characters find it?

Who or what is on the other side of the door?

What happens next?

How does the story end?

Now word-process your story.

Check your spelling.

Next step
- Using a drawing program, draw your mystery door. Put the door on a web page with a message that will make visitors want to click on it.
- Hyperlink your story text to the door.

Internet Projects for Primary Schools
Creating a Web Site
© A & C Black 2002

Science quiz

You are going to write a science quiz for a web page. Choose a science topic that you have studied recently.

Topic _____

Write six true statements related to this topic. Then rewrite the statements, changing details to make them false.

True statement

An acorn grows on an oak tree.

False statement

An acorn grows on a horse chestnut tree.

Number	True statement	False statement
1		
2		
3		
4		
5		
6		

Write your science quiz on a web page. Ask the reader to click 'True' or 'False' for each statement. Use some true statements and some false statements.

Next step
- Create hyperlinks to the quiz answers. For the false statements, include the correct versions in the answers.

Internet Projects for Primary Schools
Creating a Web Site
© A & C Black 2002

Make a fun web page

Plan a fun page for your school web site. Here are some ideas to help you get started.

Jokes
What do you call a man with a *seagull* on his head?

Cliff!

Funny stories

Puzzles
Science wordsearch

Tongue-twisters

She sells sea shells on the sea shore . . .

Quiz questions
(click to find the answer)
What is the capital city of the USA?
(Washington DC)

Anagrams
lahew whale

Find the rhyming pairs
bread and cheese → legs
bacon and eggs → knees

Next step
- Create your fun web page. Add any other ideas you can think of.
- Add a button to your page so that when people click on it, they hear laughter. This should make them laugh, too!

Click me – I can make you laugh!

83

SECTION 5:
RECOMMENDED WEB SITES

In this section you will find addresses of recommended web sites the authors have used personally and in training sessions with teachers. Each URL is for a website's home page. You may have to click a further link or more to find exactly what you want.

Most good web sites provide a direct e-mail link so that you can quickly contact them. Once the link is clicked, it will open *Outlook Express* in the usual way and will present you with a new e-mail screen into which to type your message.

Category	Type	URL	Notes
Downloads			
If your school service provider does not regularly upgrade your software, or if you work from home, here are the web sites from which you can download upgrades at no cost.			
	Internet Explorer®	www.microsoft.com/windows	Browsers upgrades and add-ons
	Netscape®	www.netscape.com	The other main browser
	Shareware	www.shareware.com	Links to other download sites
Educational			
Useful sites for general use of computers in the classroom.			
	Beginner's Centre	www.northernwebs.com/bc	A user's guide to the Internet
	Eduweb/Learning Alive	www.eduweb.co.uk,	
		www.learningalive.co.uk	Research Machine's gateway site
	Microsoft	www.microsoft.com/education	Classroom resources
	Becta	www.becta.org.uk/index.html	
Experts			
	Pitsco	www.askanexpert.com	Where children can 'ask the expert'
Government strategies, curricula and qualifications			
Official sites for details of the national curriculum, schemes of work and standards.			
	Curriculum 2000	www.curriculum2000.co.uk	Curriculum 2000 for UK schools
	DfEE	www.dfee.gov.uk	Department of Education
	National Curriculum	www.nc.uk.net	National Curriculum online
	Standards	www.standards.dfee.gov.uk	Literacy/Numeracy/Schemes
	VTC – England	www.vtc.ngfl.gov.uk	Virtual Teachers Centre: England
	VTC – Scotland VTC	www.svtc.org.uk	Virtual Teachers Centre: Scotland
	VTC – Cymru	www.vtccymru.ngfl.wales.gov.uk	Virtual Teachers Centre: Wales
Parents			
These sites offer additional resources that you may need for special downloads (plug-ins) to function properly.			
	DfEE Parents Centre	www.parents.dfee.gov.uk	Information and links
	Schoolzone	www.schoolzone.co.uk	Information and links
Plug-ins			
	Quicktime™	www.apple.com	To play video clips
	RealPlayer®	www.real.com	For online stores and radio stations
	Shockwave®	www.macromedia.com	To display 'Flash' animations properly
		www.timecast.com	Real Audio sites and live concerts

Qualifications
Sites offering educational resources.

OCR	www.ocr.org.uk	Oxford, Cambridge & RSA

Safety issues

Superhighway Safety	www.epals.com	
	www.safety.ngfl.gov.uk	

Search Engines
Directories and indexes for starting keyword searches.

Alta Vista®	www.altavista.com	
AskJeeves™	www.ask.com	Question-based
Ask Jeeves for kids	www.ajkids.com	Question-based kids search
Excite	www.excite.co.uk	UK-based general search
Google®	www.google.com	
HotBot®	www.hotbot.com	
Lycos®	www.lycos.com	
Magellan	www.magellan.excite.com	Popular web Directory
UK Plus	www.ukplus.co.uk	UK-based general search
Yahoo UK/Ireland®	www.yahoo.co.uk	UK-based general search
Yahooligans	www.yahooligans.com	Yahoo's kids search

Software
Websites from where software can be downloaded.

Becta Software	www.besd.becta.org.uk	
Compression	www.winzip.com	Winzip® for Windows
Shared	www.shareware.com	Software on a shared basis
Softease	www.textease.com	DTP, Database, Spreadsheet package

Special Needs
These sites offer advice and resources for SEN.

DfEE ICT support	www.dfee.gov.uk/sen	SEN links etc.
NASEN	www.nasen.org.uk	National Association for Special Educational Needs
BDA	www.bda-dyslexia.org.uk	British Dyslexia Association
RNIB	www.rnib.org.uk	Royal National Institute for the Blind
NAGC	www.rmplc.co.uk/orgs/nagc	National Association for Gifted Children

Teachers
Web sites offering a range of cross-curricular ideas and resources.

AskJeeves for . . .	www.ajschools.com/teachers	Useful resources and ideas
BBC Education	www.bbc.co.uk/education/schools	Home page with numerous links
Click Teaching	www.clickteaching.com	Useful resources and ideas
Educate the Children	www.educate.org.uk/teacher_zone	Useful ideas and information
ICTteachers	www.icteachers.co.uk/	Useful resources and ideas
ICT toolbox	http://crduk.extra.bt.com/ict/toolbox	BTs school resources site
Kent LEA	www.kented.org.uk/ngfl	LEA site with ideas and resources
Northern Grid	www.northerngrid.org	Northern LEA Consortium
Schoolzone	www.schoolzone.co.uk	Ideas & Information for teachers and parents
School Express	www.freeworksheets.com	American site with free worksheets
Spot Pages	www.freenetpages.co.uk	Key Stage1 resources and ideas
Stockport LEA	www.stockportmbc.gov.uk	LEA site with ideas and resources
Sunshine Online	www.literacyhour.co.uk/index.html	Simple ideas for lessons
Teaching Ideas	www.teachingideas.co.uk	Ideas and resources including ICT
VTC – England	www.timeplan.com	Virtual Teachers Centre – England
VTC – Scotland	www.svtc.org.uk	Virtual Teachers Centre – Scotland
VTC – Cymru	www.vtccymru.ngfl.wales.gov.uk	Virtual Teachers Centre – Wales
Webby Awards	www.webbyawards.com	View 'Best web site' award winners
Welcome to the web	www.teachingideas.co.uk	Excellent Internet activities

SECTION 6:
AT-A-GLANCE GUIDES

This section contains a basic checklist of computer skills and an explanation of jargon words used in this book. You may find it useful to make copies of pages 86–87 for posting in the classroom, computer room or at home.

What basic skills do I need?

USING THIS CHART

Here we have listed the skills needed to use computers efficiently and confidently in the classroom or at home. Go through the list, ticking each item if you know it or as you learn it.

You may also want to photocopy these pages and use them as a record of your pupils' progress.

Your PC
- [ ] Turn on and start up the computer
- [ ] Know your way around the keyboard
- [ ] Load and use a floppy disk, CD-ROM
- [ ] Turn on and set up a printer

Mouse Skills
- [ ] Use a mouse to select icons
- [ ] Use a mouse to drag and drop objects
- [ ] Use a mouse to open and close windows
- [ ] Single-click and double-click to open applications (programs)

The Task Bar
- [ ] Find the task bar on the desktop
- [ ] Use the task bar to run more than one program and switch between programs
- [ ] Click on the system tray on the task bar

The Start Button
- [ ] Click on the *Start* button on the task bar to open the *Start* menu
- [ ] Launch programs from the *Start* menu
- [ ] Use the *Start* menu to shut down

Desktop Icons
- [ ] Double-click on an icon to start a program
- [ ] Drag and drop icons around the desktop and rearrange them to tidy the desktop
- [ ] Double-click on an icon to open another window

Desktop Windows
- [ ] Move a window by dragging on the title bar
- [ ] Use the *Close* button
- [ ] Use the *Minimise* and *Restore* buttons
- [ ] Restore a window from the task bar

Disks, Folders, Files
- [ ] Name and save a file on to the hard drive
- [ ] Transfer work from a floppy disk
- [ ] Choose a file from a folder

Internet Projects for Primary Schools
Creating A Web Site
© A & C Black 2002

Disks, Folders, Files (continued)	☐ Create and name a folder
	☐ Click on a drive to see the files and folders
	☐ Save work in appropriately named files
	☐ Retrieve saved files from folders
	☐ Add, change and re-save a file
Information Backup	☐ Establish a routine of backing up work
	☐ Copy files on to floppy disks
	☐ Store back-up disks in a safe place
My Computer	☐ Find the *My Computer* icon
	☐ Double-click on the *My Computer* icon to look at the drives
	☐ Double-click to look at the *Control Panel*
	☐ Close the *My Computer* window
The Recycle Bin	☐ Delete an old work file in the *My Computer* window
	☐ Double-click on the *Recycle Bin* to see what is stored there temporarily
	☐ Restore a file held in the *Recycle Bin*
	☐ Permanently delete a file
Control Panel	☐ Find and launch the *Control Panel* window from the *Start* menu
	☐ Select the mouse icon in the *Control Panel* to change its speed
	☐ Close the *Control Panel* window
Printers	☐ Check the printer is on and ready to use
	☐ Use the *Print Preview* option
	☐ Use the *Quick Print* button
	☐ Print out more than one copy using the *Print* dialogue boxes
	☐ Choose one page from a longer document to print out
E-mail and the Internet	☐ Log on to the Internet
	☐ Send an e-mail
	☐ Read an e-mail from your inbox
	☐ Store an e-mail address in the address book
	☐ Visit a web site by entering its address
	☐ Bookmark a web site to explore later
	☐ Log off from the Internet

IT PAYS TO PRACTISE:

- Mouse skills such as clicking and dragging

- Navigating the desktop and knowing where to find:
  ▲ the floppy disk drive
  ▲ CD-ROM drive
  ▲ *My Computer*
  ▲ *My Documents*
  ▲ *My Briefcase*
  ▲ the *Recycle Bin*
  ▲ the applications

- Handling windows:
  ▲ dragging
  ▲ re-sizing/minimising
  ▲ scrolling
  ▲ closing down

- Routine 'housekeeping' – creating a useful filing system with folders and files organised systematically.
  Using e-mail, create folders for incoming and outgoing mail to fellow teachers, pupils, your headteacher and the LEA.

- Saving across a network and backing up files as a regular precaution

- Loading a printer with paper, clearing paper jams and changing ink cartridges.

87

Website Planner

This is not an exhaustive list, but a step-by-step guide to the kind of questions a web site planner or organiser should be considering with other colleagues and groups of pupils. The planner should be used in conjunction with the step-by-step advice given in Section 2.

PREPARATION AND PLANNING

Checked

DEALING WITH YOUR ISP | Is there a monthly fee or a start-up charge? ☐

Try visiting the host company's own site and check how long it takes for their pages to download.

Will you have plenty of free Internet access time to upload and edit your web site? ☐

Is there 24-hour technical support by phone or e-mail? ☐

Will you get at least five free e-mail addresses? ☐

Can a web site be quickly uploaded or downloaded to the host computer? ☐

AUDIENCE – WHO IS THE WEB SITE FOR?

Pupils ☐   Parents ☐   Teachers ☐

Governors ☐   Inspectors ☐   Other schools ☐

Clients ☐

BE CAREFUL about displaying private addresses or telephone numbers for anyone to see.

Would anyone else be interested?

CONTRIBUTORS AND COPYRIGHT

Just me? ☐   Pupils ☐   Parents ☐

Teachers ☐   Governors ☐   Local people ☐

These are the regular contributors. You should also consider other contributors on specialist subjects of interest.

Would anyone else be interested in contributing to your web site?

Have you made everyone involved aware of copyright issues?

CONTENT – WHAT IS THE WEB SITE FOR?

Advertising the school ☐   Timetable details ☐

Term dates ☐   Displaying children's work ☐

Don't be over-ambitious. It's better to have a simple, workable web site first and then expand.

Listing meetings and events ☐   Tests results ☐

Curriculum details ☐   Links to other schools ☐

What should you concentrate on first?

SOME CLASSROOM ACTIVITIES

Have the pupils looked critically at web sites on the Internet? ☐

Have the pupils started to collect photographs and images ready to use in your designs? ☐

Have you created clearly identified folders ready to store these resources? ☐

Internet Projects for Primary Schools
Creating A Web Site
© A & C Black 2002

> It's important to get everyone involved thinking about the shape and structure of your web site and web pages before getting to grips with the software.

Have the pupils created designs for their web pages? ☐

Have the pupils identified the audiences for your web site? ☐

Have the pupils written an introduction to your web site incorporating key words for hypertext links? ☐

Have the pupils investigated how search engines work? ☐

Have pupils been chosen to work in the editorial team? ☐

WEB-AUTHORING AND FTP SOFTWARE

Do we already have one of the web-authoring packages on our network? ☐

Could the package be introduced and used across the school for a range of purposes? ☐

Can we see it in operation at another school or LEA Centre? ☐

How long will it take a teacher to learn the basics of this package? ☐

Is it easy to show someone else how to use it, especially pupils and staff ? ☐

Does it come with a good manual and helpful examples and resources? ☐

Does it have any good online tutorials? ☐

Is it suitable for a full range of abilities, including special needs? ☐

Is it recommended by your LEA and supported with training? ☐

Is the web site easily uploaded? OR How will it be uploaded to the Internet? ☐

Is it easy to change the web pages for updating? ☐

PLANNING AND DESIGNING A WEB SITE TEMPLATE

Paper planning templates	Have you prepared paper templates of your own?	☐
	Will you be using prepared paper templates (see pages 90–92)?	☐
Shape and structure	Have you decided on the structure of your web site?	☐
	Have you decided on the number and type of content areas?	☐
	Have you settled on what page shape will you be using?	☐
Page size and background	Have you settled on the focus of the main areas of your pages?	☐
	Have you decided where the main area links will be?	☐
Alignment	Has everyone involved practised alignment in classroom activities?	☐
	Has everyone involved practised it in your software package?	☐
Repetition	Do all the pages have the same general appearance?	☐
	Do your chosen text sizes and colours complement one another?	☐
Contrast	Are all the related objects like hot spot links clearly grouped?	☐
Proximity	Are all these groups clearly separated from each other?	☐
	Is there enough clear space on your pages?	☐
	Have you now been able to draw up a template design?	☐

89

90

Web page layout

Web site template 1

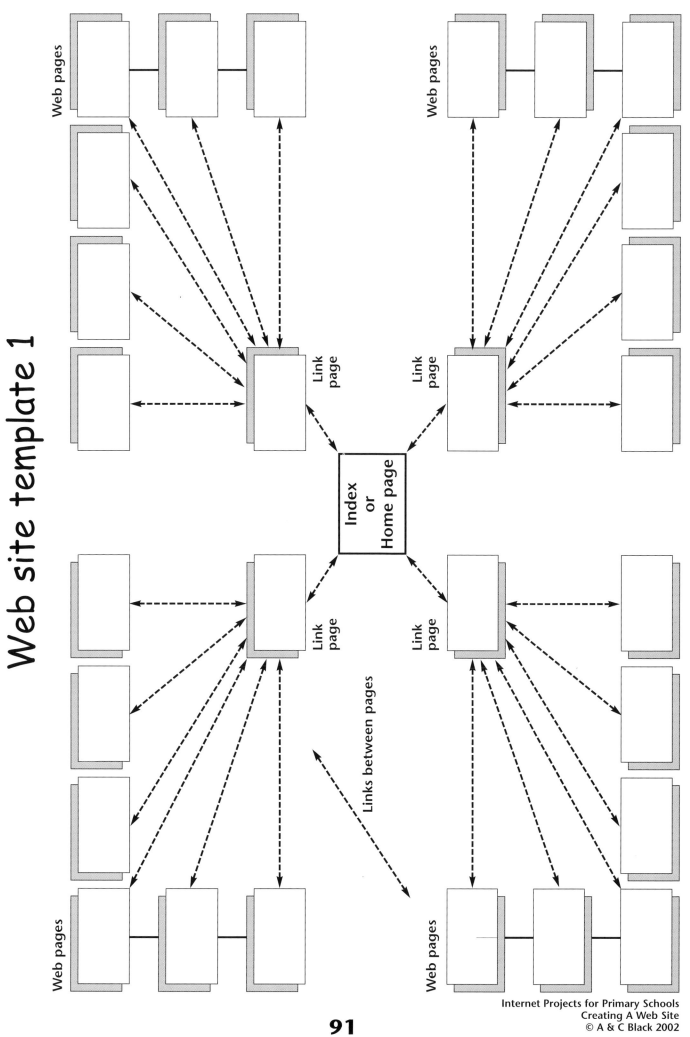

Web pages

Link page

Link page

Index or Home page

Link page

Link page

Web pages

Links between pages

Internet Projects for Primary Schools
Creating A Web Site
© A & C Black 2002

Web site template 2

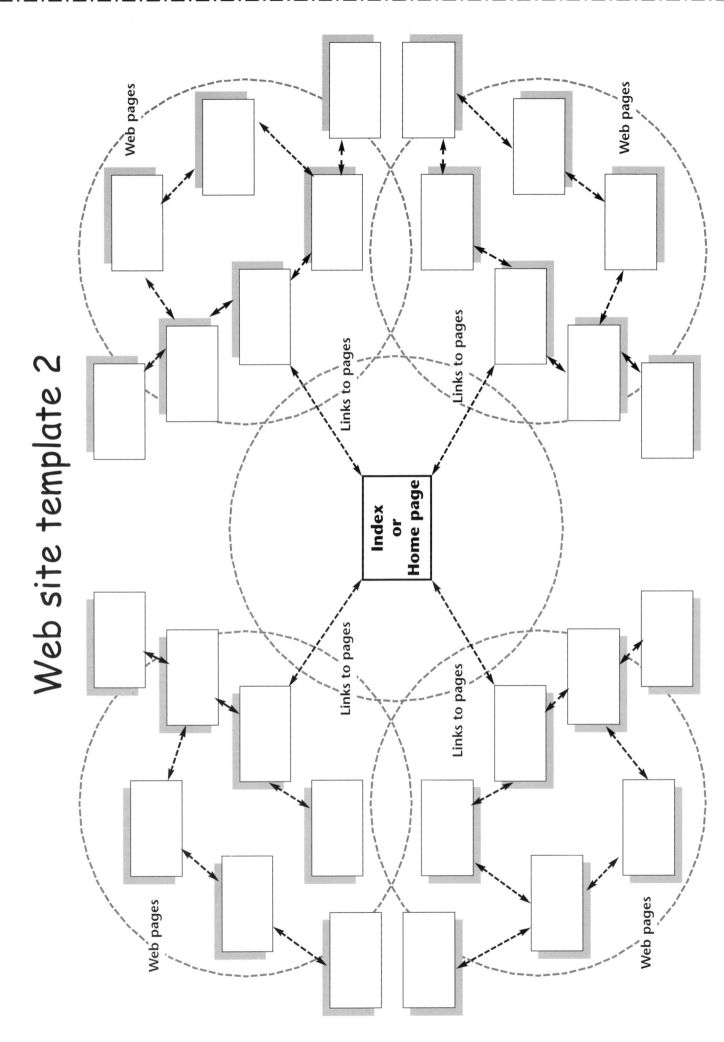

GLOSSARY

access provider A company that lets you connect to the Internet by dialling into their computer. *See also* Internet Service Provider.

address On the Internet, the precise location of a particular web site or web page, that is also known as its URL. *See also* URL.

ADSL Short for 'asymmetric digital subscriber line'. A high-speed permanent connection to the Internet. *See also* ISDN.

animated GIF Two or more image files combined to create a very simple moving picture or animation. *See also* GIF.

application A software program designed to let you do particular kinds of task on your computer. A word-processing application, for example, is designed for working on screen with words but no pictures.

back-ups Copies of computer files kept on storage disks, not your hard disk. It is vital to make and keep back-ups in case files are lost or corrupted. *See also* floppy disk.

bandwidth Measurement of the amount of information that can be transferred over an Internet telephone connection.

bin An area on your hard disk where deleted files stay until a decision is made to get rid of them. On an Apple Macintosh computer the bin is called the Wastebasket.

bookmarks *Netscape Navigator*'s way of storing direct links to the addresses of favourite web sites. See also '*Favorites*'.

browser The vital piece of Internet software for viewing pages from the World Wide Web. The two most popular browsers are *Internet Explorer* and *Netscape Navigator*.

cache A folder on your hard drive in which your browser stores all the files it downloads from the World Wide Web (in case you want to view those pages again).

CD-ROM Short for 'compact disc, read-only memory'. Used for games, information and software installation, this sort of compact disc cannot be recorded over (hence 'read-only').

clip art Images that have been created by someone else for you to use on computer.

clipboard An area on your hard disk where anything you copy or cut from a file is temporarily stored until it is pasted into another file (or another place in the same file).

cookie A small text file that some web sites store on your computer so that they know who you are next time you visit.

copy, cut, paste A set of really useful editing tools found within many kinds of programs including word processors and browsers.

copyright Laws that protect text and images from unlawful copying.

cyberspace A word coined by William Gibson in his novel *Necromancer*. It is used as a very generalised term for the Internet and everything that comes with it.

Data Protection Act Act of law designed to protect individuals from misuse of information held on computer or file about them. Find out more about it from: **www.open.gov.uk/dpr/dprhome.htm.**

database A collection of stored records which might include text, images and/or numbers.

digital camera A camera that does not use photographic film that needs processing, but instead captures and stores images as digital files. These files can be transferred on to your computer for display, printing out, sending in an e-mail attachment or posting on a web page.

domain name The unique name given to every web site on the Internet such as: **www.sitetraining.com**

download To copy computer data from one computer to another (or to a disk), possibly via the Internet. The opposite term is uploading.

drag, drop Moving icons, text or objects around on screen. To drag something, click the mouse button over it and move the mouse with the button held down. Drop the object in the right place by releasing the mouse button.

DTP Short for 'desktop publishing'. Describes applications that combine word-processing functions with image-handling functions.

export To send data from one computer program to another. For example, you can export an image that you have found on the Internet in a format that you could use in a DTP program.

FAQ Short for 'frequently-asked questions'. These – along with their answers – are often displayed on a web site or in a newsgroup.

favorites A menu in Microsoft's *Internet Explorer* browser (and a corresponding folder on your hard disk) that contains shortcuts to web sites that you visit regularly. *See also* Bookmarks.

file format The type of file. For example, a JPEG is a file format that is suitable for images, whereas Text Only is one format suitable for words.

file management Organising your computer files according to a sensible, user-friendly system. This is especially important when the use of a computer is shared.

floppy disk A storage device on which you can back up small files (usually up to 1.44 Mb). Despite its name, a floppy disk is square and hard – the round, floppy bit is hidden inside.

font A style of lettering, for example **bold,** *italic* or roman.

freeware Software that you do not have to pay for.

gateway A program or device that acts as a kind of translator between two networks so that they can communicate with each other.

GIF Short for 'graphic interchange format'. One of the two most common file formats for graphics used on the Internet. *See also* JPEG.

graphics General term describing images created and stored on computers.

graphing program A program that will create charts and graphs from the data entered.

history list A list stored by your browser showing recently visited web sites so that you can see where you have been and revisit sites easily.

home page (1) The page displayed by your browser when you start it up, or when you click the *Home* button. (2) The first page (or main contents page) of a web site.

host A computer connected directly to the Internet, usually all the time, such as your Internet Service Provider's computer. The host machine allows other computers to connect to it.

housekeeping Regular computer system maintenance such as deleting out-of-date files, organising files into directories or folders, making back-up copies of files and emptying the Recycle Bin.

HTML Short for 'hypertext mark-up language'. The computer code used to create web pages and links.

http Short for 'hypertext transport protocol'. Often forms the beginning of a web site address or URL.

icon A small picture on screen that represents a function, program, file or folder. You can click on an icon to jump to a different place or to perform a task.

ICT Short for 'Information and Communication Technology', now one of the core subjects of the National Curriculum.

image map A single image divided into several 'hot' areas and placed on a web page. Each area will take you to a different page or file when clicked.

import To receive some computer data from another program or storage device.

Internet A gigantic network of computers, all linked together and able to exchange information, that no one completely owns or controls. Sometimes, its name is shortened to 'the Net'.

Internet Explorer The name of Microsoft's browser software. *See also* Browser.

Internet Service Provider (ISP) A company that allows you to connect to the Internet by dialling into their host machine. *See also* host.

Intranet A network of computers that are linked together using Internet technology, but which are private and not accessible to everyone. Many educational institutions have an Intranet.

ISDN Short for 'integrated services digital network'. A kind of telephone line that can handle (transport) lots of complex data, including large images, very speedily.

JPEG Short for 'joint photographic experts group'. One of the two most common file formats for pictures used on the Internet. *See also* GIF.

keyword, key phrase A word or phrase that you type into a search engine, so that it can look for any web sites that may contain information relevant to that word or phrase.

log off To disconnect from the Internet, so that your browser breaks the link with the host computer.

log on To connect to the Internet, by telling your browser to dial up and form a link with the host computer. Often, you have to identify yourself at the start of a session, by typing in a username and password. *See also* username.

menu The list of possible options in a program.

mirror site An exact copy of a web site, located on a different computer.

modem A device that that allows a computer to send and receive digital information down analogue phone lines. It may be inside or outside the computer.

multimedia A mix of differently formatted information, such as text, still images, sound files and animation, such as those stored on a CD-ROM.

netiquette Term used to describe accepted rules of behaviour on the Internet (formed from 'Net' and 'etiquette'). An example of bad netiquette is typing e-mails in capital letters, which looks like you are shouting.

network Two or more computers that are connected to each other by cables, or that can be connected to each other via modems and telephone lines, so that they can swap data.

newsgroup A group of Internet users that swap ideas and opinions on a shared, common interest.

offline Not connected to the Internet but able to continue working on files. *See also* online.

online Connected to the Internet. *See also* offline.

portal An Internet site that has a search engine and a directory of links to other websites. Portals make good starting points for Internet searches.

QCA Short for 'Qualifications and Curriculum Authority'.

qwerty Description of the traditional keyboard arrangement, as on a typewriter's keys: the letters 'q', 'w', 'e', 'r', 't' and 'y' are the first letter keys to appear at the top left.

RAM Short for 'random access memory'. Short-term memory used by your computer.

refresh, reload Forcing the browser to download a web page again by clicking a tool bar button labelled *Refresh* (in *Internet Explorer*) or *Reload* (in *Netscape Navigator*). This can be useful if the page seems to have 'frozen'.

ROM Short for 'read-only memory'. A way of storing information so that it can be read very fast, but not changed in any way, for example on a CD-ROM. *See also* CD-ROM.

search engine A website that maintains an index of other web pages and sites, allowing you to search for pages on a particular subject by entering keywords or key phrases. Examples include *Yahoo* and *Google*.

server A computer that provides a service, such as hosting many web sites, or connecting to your service provider's mail server when you decide to send or receive e-mail.

service provider A company that gives you access to the Internet by letting you dial in to their computer. This may be an Internet Service Provider or an online service.

URL Short for 'uniform resource locator'. The unique address of a website or web page.

username The unique name that you use when using your computer in order to identify yourself.

virus A piece of computer code that can attach itself to programs or files on your computer and corrupt or delete them. To avoid 'catching' a virus, check any new files you download using anti-virus software.

WAP Short for 'wireless application protocol'. Describes web-like pages written in a language called WML (similar to HTML) that can be downloaded into WAP-enabled mobile phones and pagers.

web page A single document (usually with **.htm** or **.html** at the end of its name) that is a tiny part of the Internet. Web pages may contain text, images and links to other web pages.

web server A computer or program dedicated to storing Web pages and transmitting them to your computer to be viewed in your browser.

web site A collection of related web pages and files, usually created by or belonging to a single individual or company, and located on the same web server.

word bank A list of words, phrases and pictures that children can click on, rather than typing in the words for themselves. Word banks can be created in some educational software, such as *Textease*, and cut down on errors due to mispellings.

word processor A computer program that allows the user to input text and edit it.

World Wide Web A vast collection of documents and files stored on web servers. The documents are known as web pages and are created using a language called HTML. All these pages and files are linked together by a common language called hypertext.

www Short for 'World Wide Web'. Often found at the beginning of a web address or URL.

INDEX